What Designers Kno

What Designers Know

Bryan Lawson

AMSTERDAM • BOSTON • HEIDELBERG • LONDON • NEW YORK • OXFORD
PARIS • SAN DIEGO • SAN FRANCISCO • SINGAPORE • SYDNEY • TOKYO

Architectural Press is an imprint of Elsevier

ELSEVIER

Architectural
Press

Architectural Press
An imprint of Elsevier
Linacre House, Jordan Hill, Oxford OX2 8DP
30 Corporate Drive, Burlington, MA 01803

First published 2004

British Library Cataloguing in Publication Data
A catalogue record for this book is available from the British Library

Library of Congress Cataloguing in Publication Data
A catalogue record for this book is available from the Library of Congress

ISBN 0 7506 6448 7

For information on all Architectural Press publications
visit our website at www.architecturalpress.com

Typeset by Newgen Imaging Systems (P) Ltd., Chennai, India
Printed and bound in Meppel, The Netherlands by Krips bv

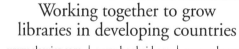

Working together to grow
libraries in developing countries

www.elsevier.com | www.bookaid.org | www.sabre.org

ELSEVIER   BOOK AID
International   Sabre Foundation

Contents

Preface

The physician can bury his mistakes, but the architect can only advise his client to plant vines.

Frank Lloyd Wright

The great American architect Frank Lloyd Wright was quoted in the *New York Times* (4 October, 1953). In the litigious climate of today his comment is unlikely to gain much sympathy from any disgruntled clients of designers. But the essence of his aphorism remains as penetratingly perceptive now as it was then. Designers commit themselves very publicly to ideas that often with the hindsight gained by the passage of time look poor or even absurd. Architects in particular have come in for some pretty bad press recently as a result. At least industrial designers see their products fade away in response to the market but buildings have a nasty habit of hanging around advertising the misjudgements of their architects.

Consider then, dear reader, the fate of authors of books about design. Not only does the book remain on the library shelves but we also have the misfortune to have our work imprinted with its initial date of publication. This rather sneakily leaps out of the page at you whenever it is referenced by others kind enough to have found it of some value in their own studies. To begin with this seems flattering but as the years go by it becomes a constant reminder of the inexorable passage of time.

My first book, *How Designers Think*, was written an alarmingly long time ago (Lawson, 1980), and if I were starting to write it now I would probably do so in quite a different way. But it has been in print ever since, and has passed through several editions as ideas have developed and more research has been done (Lawson, 1997). This book started life as yet another edition but it gradually became apparent that there was now much more to say than the original structure of *How Designers Think* was capable of accommodating.

So this book might usefully be seen as a companion volume to *How Designers Think*. We understand design a great deal better than we did when that book was first published. People have written about their own experiences of designing for centuries and a few have tried to generalize, but design theory as a serious subject on the global stage is perhaps no more than four or five decades old. There is clearly much yet to learn but we now think we know a very considerable amount about designing.

The field of knowledge had its origins in what was really known as design methodology. Those early contributions were much more in the style of deterministic methods and techniques and they were largely prescriptive. We have moved on considerably from there to a much deeper investigation and much more descriptive work. *How Designers Think* concentrated on the nature of design problems and the processes of designing. This book is more about the rather special kind of knowledge upon which designers rely and manipulate when practising their art. It will not discuss the whole range of issues that might be currently thought to be relevant to an understanding of the design process and the two books taken together offer a more complete picture of my position.

The book begins, however, with some material that overlaps with its companion as we map out the nature of designing in order to explore why design knowledge is rather unusual and special and then examine ways of investigating it. Of course design knowledge itself is invisible and so we then proceed to explore it through its common manifestations. This includes the drawings that designers make not only as they proceed with individual projects but also as they acquire and develop the knowledge upon which they rely. It includes the tricky question of the problems that designers have in relating to the newer tools of computer-aided design. Perhaps by rubbing up against such tools and finding them lacking we can learn something of the kinds of knowledge that designers need in order to work. Design is most often a social activity when carried out professionally. It involves teams of designers, specialist consultants and of course clients and other interested parties. This leads us on to examine the conversations these players have as design progresses as yet another way of revealing the nature of the knowledge they use. After piecing the argument together so far we then look at the nature of expertise in design. What is it that marks out the really successful designers? Do they know something that the rest of us do not, or maybe do they know the same things in different ways?

Of course all these questions were around back in 1980 when I first wrote *How Designers Think*. But then we had little evidence about the actual practice of design and about how the skills are acquired both academically and professionally. We had a very limited understanding of the nature of design problems. We knew design was a simultaneously frustrating and yet intellectually rewarding occupation, but we had little understanding of why. Today design still holds many mysteries but we have now gathered a considerable body of evidence about its nature. In particular we have been fortunate to see investigators coming at it from many different angles. In this book you will find data gathered or arguments developed by psychologists, sociologists, philosophers, linguists, anthropologists, cognitive scientists, computer scientists and of course by designers themselves. The nature of the knowledge that designers work with and the ways in which they manipulate it remain fertile grounds of study not just so we may learn more about design but that we may also learn to respect all these great traditions of enquiry. Design must be one of the most interdisciplinary of subjects. It often sits uncomfortably in the old-fashioned structures that many of our great universities, including my own, use to divide up knowledge. A study of design above all else perhaps teaches us to challenge those structures, whether they still help us or perhaps more often hinder our investigations.

The nature of design knowledge is both fascinating and complex. Of course a study of this may help any aspiring designer, but ultimately practising designers come to understand the nature of this knowledge implicitly and demonstrate this understanding through their actions. But there are many others who may not gain that implicit understanding since it is generally only acquired through the repeated practice of design. They may find that a study of what designers know may reveal some quite surprising and valuable insights enabling them to interface far more effectively with designers. Those who work with and rely upon designers such as clients, those who commission design, the users of design, legislators who govern design or set standards and practices within which it must operate. All of these and many others can so easily damage the delicate process of designing and thus the quality of the end product without even being aware of their impact. However, it also turns out that a study of what designers know challenges our more conventional understanding of what makes good knowledge in ways that might be of interest and value to those in the information and cognitive sciences.

Many people have been kind enough over the years to tell me how other books of mine have interested or helped them. Some too have obviously found them frustrating and even irritating. I hope that this new book too may help a few readers to develop their own ideas and understandings, but no doubt it will not be long before I wish for the literary equivalent of Frank Lloyd Wright's vines to start growing again.

Bryan Lawson

Acknowledgements

I am indebted to many colleagues and others who over the years have discussed ideas in this book. In particular the many scholars who have contributed to the Design Thinking Research Symposia and the Creativity and Cognition Conferences. I am also grateful to many research students and members of my research group. In particular Faisal Agabani, Steven Roberts, Tami Belhadj, Joongseuk Ryu, Alice Pereira, Abu Hasan Ismail, Loke Shee Ming, Marcia Pereira, Rodzyah Yunus, Mohammed Yusoff, Rashid Embi, Ahmed Bakerman, Abu Bakar, Alexandre Menezes. I am also greatly indebted to the many experienced and talented designers who have been gracious enough to discuss their thinking and knowledge with me. In particular they include Richard Burton, Santiago Calatrava, Jim Glymph, Herman Hertzberger, Eva Jiricna, Jimmy Lim, Richard MacCormac, John Outram, Ian Ritchie, Richard Seymour, Robert Venturi and Denise Scott Brown, Michael Wilford, Ken Yeang.

Illustrations

All photographs and drawings by the author unless otherwise stated.
Figs 4.1, 4.2, 4.9, 4.10, 4.11 Ken Yeang, T.R. Hamzah and Yeang Sdn Bhd, Kuala Lumpur, Malaysia
Fig. 4.3 Michael Wilford, James Stirling and Michael Wilford, London, UK
Fig. 4.4 John Outram, John Outram Associates, London, UK
Figs 4.5, 5.3 Santiago Calatrava, Santiago Calatrava, Zurich, Switzerland and Paris, France
Figs 4.7, 4.8 Frank Gehry and Jim Glymph, Gehry Partners LLP, Los Angeles, USA
Fig. 4.13 Eva Jiricna, Eva Jiricna Architects, London
Figs 5.1, 5.2, 6.4, 6.5 Robert Venturi, Venturi Scott Brown and Associates, Philadelphia, USA
Fig. 9.1 and front cover Candi Lawson (at a very young age)

Uncovering design knowledge

A designerly way of knowing.

Nigel Cross

Knowledge comes, but wisdom lingers.

Alfred, Lord Tennyson

Is there such a thing as 'design knowledge'?

Describing what designers know is not an easy task. At a recent forum on architectural education one speaker challenged the conference to say what architects did. An easy question to answer you may think but not one of the experienced practitioners and educationalists present was brave enough to take up the challenge. No one felt able to offer a succinct description that they were confident would be widely agreed upon and yet describe the work of all architects. It is quite possible to find two people who call themselves architects and yet hardly share any of their daily tasks. The more generic question about what designers do is even more difficult to answer simply and successfully. This book is not about architecture or specifically about architects, nor is it a book that will tell you how to design. Rather it will attempt to develop part of what has to be a rather long answer to some very short questions. What is it that designers know? Does design knowledge involve a special way of knowing? How do designers acquire and make use of their knowledge? In this book then we will explore the common features we can detect in the kinds of knowledge designers rely upon and try to explain why they are indeed rather special and in some ways rather unconventional.

To begin with we can see that designing is not alone in being so difficult to pin down. We could, for example, ask 'What do farmers do?' It is perfectly possible to find two farmers who share almost no common activities in carrying out their work. One might be a hill farmer who tends sheep while the other might be an arable lowland farmer growing wheat. We have no difficulty in agreeing that both of these two fine and honest fellows are farmers and yet they do quite different jobs. 'Well', you might say, 'the common factor is easy to see, they both grow food in one way or another. So the answer is that farmers grow food.' Now this might be true in this case, but the hill farmer may turn out only to breed sheep for their wool and never sends them to market, so not all farmers grow food. The definition is thus not as easy as it may at first seem.

In *How Designers Think* (Lawson, 1997) I listed many definitions of design and found them mostly wanting in some way and I shall not repeat the exercise here. However, let us briefly follow the farming example by comparing two designers. One might be a fashion designer creating exclusive, expensive and perhaps largely impractical one-off collections of clothes for the haute couture market in one of our great fashion centres such as Paris, Milan, Sao Paulo or London. Our other designer might be an architect employed by an international chain of fast food retail outlets that shall remain nameless here. Our first designer is likely to achieve success largely through originality and novelty while our second would almost certainly lose his or her job by designing anything remotely original. The haute couture world thrives on a kind of wackiness and yet also moves with a kind of global consensus, at one time conforming to this hem length and colour palette, at another time to quite different ideas. By contrast the whole notion of the multinational fast food concession is that each outlet is instantly recognizable to its patrons at all times and in all countries, cultures and climates.

So is it possible that these two designers really belong to the same basic occupational group? Can we really discuss design in such a wide-ranging way or must we always confine our analysis to one tightly defined group at a time? The answer surely must be that there are likely to be some common features or we would never have the concept of 'design' in the first place, and just like the two farmers we have no difficulty in recognizing both of our odd couple as 'designers'. However, clearly we must delve deeper into their differences and try to find a theory that allows us to position each designer in a meaningful structure that can relate one to another. That structure is surely something to do with the knowledge that the designers depend upon for their work and the skills they use to manipulate it. It is that which we shall explore here.

Expertise in design

We must also be able to explain yet another variation, which, it turns out, is at least as interesting and important. That is the level of expertise that designers have. Some designers become very successful while others may be much less so. A difficulty here is just how we define success, and in fact there are many indicators we might use. Some designers get repeated commissions, may command higher fees, have international reputations, and may influence the development of ideas in their field. So what distinguishes these outstanding or expert designers? What do they 'know' that others do not, or what skills do they have that others have not developed? The study of expertise and excellence is in itself an interesting business. In some areas of human endeavour expertise is almost certainly largely a matter of knowing more. Perhaps we might expect the best academics to have more knowledge than their less illustrious counterparts. In other fields expertise is less a matter of knowledge and more one of skill. The top football players who are transferred from one club to another perhaps across international boundaries for astronomical fees are not generally able to articulate more knowledge but clearly can execute certain skills at a higher level and more consistently than those languishing in the lower leagues. But it is not as simple as that; we also often admire a sporting star not just for the execution of a skill but also for the ability to 'see' a shot or a pass that lesser players would not have even thought of playing. This may well give us some hints about expertise that we shall find helpful later in the book. Sometimes it is neither skill nor knowledge per se that is important but a way of seeing or perceiving that may be the crucial ability in an activity. But we must delay a more full examination of expertise in design until after we have explored the range of issues involved in design knowledge.

Types of knowledge

It is now time to admit to something about the title of this book. Taken at face value the title may actually be rather misleading. This is because our everyday use of the words 'know' and 'knowledge' is often restricted to our retention and articulation of facts. But even from our very brief exploration so far it must already be apparent that there are many ways of 'knowing'. There is certainly what has been recognized as 'knowledge in action'. We may, for example, 'know' how to ride a bicycle or how to swim. Such knowledge is often hard to acquire, and even more difficult to describe or explain, and yet easy to recognize. We may also 'know' how to see or hear in particular ways. You may be able to identify a song by the Beatles or a concerto by Mozart perhaps even if you have not heard them before. Such ways of knowing how it turns out are rather important in designing. This chapter began with a quotation from that greatly influential scholar of design theory, Nigel Cross. In fact Nigel coined the phrase 'a designerly way of knowing' and used it as the title of a paper that has provoked much thinking by many others (Cross, 1982). It is now probably fair to say that there is a general consensus among researchers that there is indeed such a thing as a 'designerly way of knowing'. But just how do we find out what it is?

Ways of uncovering design knowledge

In fact there are several things we can do. They all turn out to have serious disadvantages as research tools, but we can learn something from each of them. We shall rely on all of them in this book.

First, we can simply sit and think about design knowledge. We can look at the information designers are given and the information they produce. From this we can attempt some inferences about the information they may have used to transform the inputs into the outputs. Such an approach appears simple and logical, but it turns out to be far from adequate. This is primarily because design is a creative process by its very nature. Much highly valued or successful design begins with very little external information and yet creates highly influential outputs and ideas. It seems then that the designers must have used a considerable amount of knowledge which has never been externalized or articulated.

Second, we can attempt some more rigour and put the designer in a controlled situation and observe him or her under empirical conditions. This may represent a very respectable form of research but it is extremely difficult to conduct with a sufficient degree of realism to be relevant to what those designers actually do in practice. In fact when we carry out such experiments and ask the subjects about them they most frequently complain about two features. First, they are likely to point out that they were not able to visit the site, interrogate the client, look at parallel situations, discuss problems with the manufacturer, test aspects of the design by watching its use in real situations, or browse information sources in the way they would have chosen to. All of these and many other similar complaints suggest that in this artificial experimental world they were deprived of much information that their experience suggests might have been helpful and perhaps even crucial. Second, experimental subjects complain that they do not very often design in this way and usually do many other things at the same time and that these periods of thinking about other matters are often when they make important progress on their design projects. This suggests that they use their knowledge in ways they do not even fully understand themselves.

A third research approach allows our investigated designers to work in their natural settings and relies on simply observing them in their studios. While this offers more realism it seldom offers much useful data! Unfortunately the really interesting things that happen in the design process are hidden in designers' heads rather than being visible. It does not necessarily reveal the actual knowledge they are using although it may reveal the important sources. If we simply listen to what designers are saying or watch what they are doing we are likely to be missing the main action. Recording the events when groups of designers are at work under reasonably controlled conditions is a compromise which is increasingly popular. However, experienced groups of designers seem able to develop such important and powerful forms of verbal and visual 'shorthand' that even here the investigator may be missing very important material. Later in this book, however, we shall explore the way designers communicate in teams during the process and see what we can learn from all this.

Our fourth technique for investigating design is simply to ask designers to tell us what they know. We might try to gather this from what they write about themselves or we might interview them. Reading what designers write is rather dangerous since we have little or no guide as to how reliable and accurate this is. Actually we do perhaps have some reasons for being just a little suspicious about such data for several reasons. The first is that designers are not professional communicators through writing. Second, they may well be writing in order to promote themselves and their practices, and are thus more likely to be seeking to impress than to explain. Finally, designers are used to having to act as advocates for their work during interviews or meetings with their clients. Since by its very nature design is an activity that cannot be theoretically proved to be optimal, clients often take some convincing. Even as students, designers learn through the studio to 'sell' their ideas. My overwhelming experience of teaching design students for many years is that they tend to present their process as having been far more logical and founded on solid knowledge than it was in reality. This may not necessarily be a deliberate deceit as they may have come to believe this version of events themselves. So we must at least be cautious about what designers write about themselves when they become fully fledged professionals. Interviewing designers may be subject to all these dangers too. However, I have found that interviewing designers privately and confidentially not about individual projects but about their process in general and the knowledge they rely upon can alleviate some of these problems. Unfortunately such a technique requires considerable skill to carry out. To obtain meaningful results the researcher needs extensive knowledge of the designers and their work. This is all very time-consuming as the data gathered is often highly specific and hard to generalize. It is also hard to persuade the very best designers to subject themselves to this process, although some are much more willing to participate in interviews than to be subjects in laboratory experiments.

Our fifth and final technique for investigating design knowledge is a very indirect one and a rather recent addition to our research toolkit. We can try to simulate the design process. There are signs that cognitive scientists are beginning to invent software which can make design-like decisions. Interestingly it turns out that modelling design-like thinking challenges cognitive science in ways that many other kinds of cognition do not. However, a problem with this method is that even if we manage to develop software that appears to design and even if we can get it to produce results similar to those produced by designers we still cannot be sure that it relied upon the same kind of knowledge and used it in the same kind of way.

So we are left with a varied toolkit full of imperfect methods for investigating design. This book will rely on all of them at various points in the argument. No one technique and indeed no one piece of research can give us all the answers. Somehow we have to take it all together, with all the caveats and cautions that are appropriate and get an overall picture. That is what this book will try to do. In it we shall try to uncover the kinds of knowledge that designers use and how they bring it to bear in their process. We shall review research which is done in the field and in the laboratory. We shall examine the drawings that designers make and the conversations they hold. We shall explore the way they collaborate and interact with other designers and with their clients and users. We shall look at how they interact with computers. We shall look at research which enables us to compare how experienced and expert designers behave compared with novices and students. All these sources of information will enable us to piece together some understanding of what it is that designers know.

2

Why might design knowledge be special?

If it is true that there is an irreducible element of art in professional practice, it is also true that gifted engineers, teachers, scientists, architects, and
managers sometimes display artistry in their day-to-day practice.
Donald Schön, *The Reflective Practitioner* (1983)

You think philosophy is difficult enough, but I tell you it is nothing to the difficulty of being a good architect.

Wittgenstein

Is there a prima-facie reason to believe that design knowledge is in some way
special and therefore deserving the attention of a book such as this? Why
might we believe that design knowledge is likely to turn out to be different
or special? There are some clues that may help us answer this question. One
clue is that design education looks different to much else of what goes on in
universities around the world. In fact you can go into schools of design and see
a very similar pattern repeating time and again. This is true whether the school
is in England, The Netherlands, the USA, Australia, Malaysia or Hong Kong.
In fact it appears to be a pretty global pattern. It is true whether the school is
teaching architecture, product design, interior design or landscape design. All
these institutions seem to have understood and appreciated something that has
driven them to organize their departments and courses in certain similar ways.

Knowing by doing

And yet there is also something very hard to pin down about all this. At the
time of writing this book I have been studying the design process for around
four decades. I have read degrees in architecture and in psychology. I have
conducted studies and experiments on design. I have studied, observed and
interviewed many leading designers. I have taught in many countries and universities. I have written books and papers on the design process and attended
countless conferences on the subject. And yet! And yet I still find something
curious and slightly disturbing which is this ... Whenever I hear someone
deliver a lecture or I read a paper on the design process, somehow I can usually
tell whether or not that speaker or author is actually a designer. There seems to

be a certain kind of knowledge and understanding that it is very hard to attain in any way other than by actually designing seriously. All those schools of design understand this too and use methods of learning by doing in the 'studio' format as their primary educational tool.

I remember well early in my career teaching architecture working with a young and very talented urban sociologist on some joint studio projects. I must have infuriated the poor girl who had no previous knowledge of design at all. She would occasionally demonstrate this with some quite impractical or unrealistic suggestion about how she thought the students would work, or what we might require them to achieve. I think I probably told her that she did not understand how design worked and that we could not do it like that. Eventually her justifiable anger at my failure to explain my criticism of her overflowed and she banged the table we were working at. OK why don't you just give me the undergraduate textbook in architecture and I will go away and read it, she shouted at me. Of course my response to this was only to further inflame the situation when I tried to explain that of course there was no such text, and never would be and could not be. Design has to be learned by doing rather than by reading a textbook. I had been lucky. I had studied architecture first and then read a postgraduate degree in psychology. I did indeed go away and read the undergraduate textbook in psychology. As I recall I did so in a couple of weeks effectively skimming through a complete first degree syllabus. Now while of course I could not claim at that time to have the more comprehensive understanding I have gathered over the years I could very nearly catch up with those on my course who had read psychology as a first degree. My urban sociologist colleague's prospects of catching up with me as a designer were slight indeed by comparison. That was not due to any failing on her part or to any significant achievement on mine. Rather it tells us something about the nature of design knowledge and how it might be different from many other kinds of knowledge.

Some years ago in the UK a group of building contractors were trying to do something about the confrontational and litigious nature of the relationships between the various professions involved in delivering new buildings. They strongly advocated a common undergraduate degree should be developed (Bill, 1990). Virtually all of the schools of architecture thought the idea ridiculous and howled in protest. It appeared that perhaps the architects were being separatist, elitist or just plain awkward. But in fact their experience told them that the idea simply would not work because design knowledge has to be acquired in a special kind of way. The contractors just could not see this and the architectural educators found it very hard to explain.

Yet another clue would be the understanding that the general public has of what designers are, what they do and what they know. There is a paradox here for design is at once everyday and yet special. We all design to some extent every day. We assemble our place of work, our home, and even the way we look. We choose our cars and other belongings. We express ourselves to others through these decisions. We do all this mostly in an unselfconscious way and would find it very hard to articulate the basis on which we make many of these design-like decisions. Professional designers, however, do all these things for other people rather than just for themselves. Designers are somehow able to understand something about their clients and users that those people seem not to be able to understand about themselves. They can at times give what the British architect Sir Denys Lasdun described as 'not what he [the client] wants but what he never even dreamt of' (Lasdun, 1965). This process when played out on popular television programmes for reworking gardens or interiors of the homes of ordinary people shows how magically their lives can be interpreted and enhanced by a designer. In such popularizations of course we seldom see the failures. We must remember, however, that the dream of which Lasdun spoke so enthusiastically could also be a nightmare if the designer misunderstands the client.

All of these clues offer a similar indication. It is that there is some knowledge that designers use which is on the one hand crucial and central and yet on the other implicit, poorly understood and seldom explained.

Knowledge beyond the problem

What must be apparent from all this is that design solutions have a rather curious and complex relationship with design problems. A question we might ask here is 'How does a designer get from problem to solution?' Our answer must gradually be developed throughout the book, but we can at least begin by saying that the link is neither direct nor simple. Similarly we might ask how professionals from other sectors of activity get from their problems to their solutions. Is there some taxonomy of the problem–solution relationship that we can apply here? If so this is certainly too ambitious a project for this book, but some dimensions can at least be speculated about. It is surely apparent that designers bring a great deal into the situation that was not in the original problem, however that might be expressed.

If we explore the field of architecture then a question that might be helpful here is to establish if there is a difference between the concepts of architecture and building? Somehow in our everyday language we assume these two words to have overlapping meanings but they are certainly not coterminous. The word 'building' implies a practical unfussy approach and is often used by clients and contractors. The word 'architecture' implies some artistic aspiration and when used by an architect seems intended to indicate something on a higher level than mere 'building'. Indeed the architectural historian Nicholas Pevsner claimed that 'A bicycle shed is a building, Lincoln Cathedral is architecture'. Such an idea suggests that the humble bicycle shed has drawn on less knowledge to produce than has the great cathedral. Surely such a comparative definition will not survive too deep an examination! It must be possible to imagine an ugly cathedral and a beautiful bicycle shed. It must surely be possible to imagine a cathedral that works poorly and a bicycle shed that works well. Yet again we may think it not impossible, even if unlikely in practice, for a cathedral to be put together carelessly. It is certainly possible for a bicycle shed to be lovingly crafted. Just before working on this book I had designed and built a simple shelter in my garden in which I now sit to write when the weather permits (Fig. 2.1). I had not long previously visited the magical Indonesian island of Bali, and my garden pavilion was heavily influenced by

Figure 2.1
A humble garden shelter but suggesting evidence of the use of knowledge beyond the problem

the 'pondoks' to be found everywhere there in the rice fields. These charming shelters offer a place in which the workers may rest in the heat of the midday sun. I claim no great achievement in the design of my pavilion but even so I would argue to Pevsner that it is more then mere 'building', and has at least some of the attributes of 'architecture'. Perhaps this is because I brought knowledge to bear from outside the problem in generating my solution. This knowledge depended on my having seen things, and was highly personal in the sense that someone else could have designed an equally good if different pavilion using quite different knowledge.

The architect Edwin Lutyens described architecture as 'building with wit'. Again suggesting that architecture relies on more knowledge than building but this time not associating this distinction with a typology or a scale of construction as did Pevsner. The philosopher Wittgenstein, who became very interested in architecture, left us many interesting thoughts here. According to Wilson (1986) Wittgenstein said: 'Architecture is a gesture. Not every purposive movement of the human body is a gesture. And no more is every building designed for a purpose architecture.' This somewhat poetic and rather delightful comment lends further support to the idea that architecture has higher aspirations than mere building. In particular Wittgenstein here is again suggesting that architecture draws on a body of knowledge that lies beyond the local problem under consideration. The parallel with 'gesture' could be interpreted to refer to that body of knowledge about the special movements we call dance, and in some cases the specific body of knowledge about classical ballet. Indeed to return to Bali, there one finds a kind of dance that is extraordinarily gestural and expressive. This is far from mere movement but entirely entrancing and magical in its ability to communicate events and emotions (Fig. 2.2).

Figure 2.2
Balinese dance is largely based on highly expressive gestures

Wittgenstein seems to be suggesting to us that to understand architecture as opposed to mere building one must have some access to a similar greater body of knowledge. Others of Wittgenstein's observations show him frequently referring to communicative and expressive qualities as being pre-requisites of what he considers to be architecture: 'Where there is nothing to glorify there can be no architecture'.

Whether one goes the whole way with Wittgenstein about architecture is perhaps not central to our argument here. Our purpose here is to show that there is some higher quality depending on some identifiable body of knowledge lying outside and beyond the problem that distinguishes architecture from building. Translating this into more generic language requires us to see that design as opposed to mere problem solving requires the application of a body of knowledge not stated or necessarily even referred to in the brief. In essence then design problems of the kind we are studying in this book are not defined in such a way that any two designers trying to solve them would rely upon the same body of knowledge. Since each designer takes their own approach, each will require supporting knowledge related to that approach. Unlike problems of science there is no one commonly shared theoretical body of knowledge which can be applied to generate a solution. Goel and Pirolli (1992) make even more wide sweeping and dramatic claims: 'The kinds of knowledge that may enter into a design solution are practically limitless'.

Problems and solutions

But there is still yet another curious feature of the relationship between design problems and their solutions which suggests design may be a rather special activity. Quite simply they do not map onto each other in any logical, predictable or generally understandable way. This is most easily understood by looking at attempts to make them relate in a logical manner.

The first example is found in the early work of the design theorist Christopher Alexander. In particular we find this in his seminal work, Notes on the Synthesis of Form (Alexander, 1964), which he later revised slightly (Alexander, 1966). Alexander was troubled by the complexity of design problems and the need to break them down in manageable chunks that could be addressed by the human mind. He developed a mathematical system of decomposing design problems hierarchically into chunks that were as discrete as could be found within the overall framework. Alexander illustrated this with an approach to the design of a village. Each feature required by the brief was given a score relating it to all other features. A mathematical cluster analysis then isolated groups of sub-problems that were closely related and having minimal links to other sub-problems. The idea was that a designer could then propose solutions to each of these sub-problem clusters and then assemble all these sub-solutions into an overall solution.

The second example is found in the writing of a prominent and influential building scientist, John Page. Page (1963) proposed a method of designing based on sub-optimization and relying on a 'cumulative' approach. The example of designing a window may seem fairly trivial by comparison with Alexander's whole village but in fact this shows just how complex apparently simple design features can be. Page recognized that the window serves many purposes such as allowing in daylight, providing ventilation, affording a view and so on. It also carries with it some inherent dangers such as the risk of undesirable excessive solar gain, the transmission of noise and so on. Page suggests that the designer should first set a series of criteria for success for the window for each of these aspects of its performance. He then calls for the designer to create a series of sub-solutions or window configurations that optimize the design against each of these criteria. It then only remains to reject those solutions that do not satisfy all or enough of the criteria leaving the designer with the best overall solutions to select from.

We could cite other similar attempts from the early days of what was then called 'design methodology' having similar qualities to these two examples. Of course none of these have survived the test of time or even been known to have been used in practice seriously. There is a reported attempt to use the Alexander technique (Hanson, 1969) but even that hardly appears to have been an unqualified success. These two examples failed because they attempted to impose a structure on the problem–solution relationship in design which is simply not there. In good design we can seldom decompose the solution and point to a series of identifiable features or components and show them as uniquely solving aspects of the problem. As I showed in *How Designers Think* the delightful Georgian window was a remarkably good synthesis of daylighting, ventilation, view, privacy, structure and many other factors (Lawson, 1997). The overall pattern and shape beautifully and simultaneously manages to solve all the problems pretty well. As Simon (1973) would have said of course it is not a matter of optimizing but of what he called 'satisficing', or getting everything good enough.

Design solutions tend to be holistic

In *How Designers Think* I showed how this was true even for vernacular or what we might call pre-professional design. George Sturt's wonderful book analysing the design of the farmyard cartwheel taught us this in as charming and powerful a way as one could hope for (Sturt, 1923). He showed that the one idea of making the cartwheel dished rather than flat simultaneously solved problems of, among others, manufacture, manoeuvrability, stability, loading patterns, dealing with road ruts, and even some early planning legislation.

This idea, however, can be seen to be characteristic of much good modern professional design. The relatively humble motorway service station shown here (Fig. 2.3) has only a few basic ideas behind the concept of its design. In fact it is what we might call a 'section' building. The main design idea is the shape of the section which is then extruded to form a generally linear building. The section used here divides the roof and allows natural light deep inside the plan. The circulation of customers flows naturally down the extruded building with the servery following the line of the split roof thus marking out the public domain from the 'behind the scenes' kitchen areas. This simple device allows for the delivery of food and materials to be separate from the removal of waste as required by legislation and both of these to be separate from the circulation of customers. The split section roof can also house artificial lighting to create a similar lighting pattern at night to that from natural light in the daytime. Also here can be located the ventilation removing the smells from the kitchens before they reach the public areas. The public side of the servery is found under the highest part of the roof where the activity is most public and communal. However, the roof slopes down and produces a more intimate scale where the patrons actually eat their food. They also find themselves near a wall glazed along its full length affording a view of a quiet garden protected from the motorway by a landscaped hill. This together with the heavy sloping roof of the section and its deep overhang prevents noise from the motorway disturbing the customers as they eat. Finally we see that the section composes

Figure 2.3
A motorway service station that uses one idea of a sectional outline to solve many problems

itself in an interesting way as we arrive from the motorway and visually directs us into the appropriate entrance area. So here problems of circulation, legislation, lighting, ventilation, noise, view, scale and the creation of appropriate places are all achieved with the aid of one major idea, the shape of the building section. This is design integration. We cannot say here which bit of the building solves which bit of the problem. Solution and problem simply do not map onto each other in a way that could be predicted from the problem or from any theory. Another architect might produce a quite different design for this building that still solves all the same problems but integrates them into quite different forms and in different ways. The methods of Alexander and Page are most unlikely to lead to this kind of result. Design solutions are characteristically often holistic responses to the design problem. Somehow skilled designers must be bringing some extra knowledge to bear on the problem in order to transform it into this kind of integrated solution.

Knowledge about design problems

There is another important way in which design problems make the design situation rather special. Quite simply they are seldom ever expressed in a thorough and comprehensive way. There are two main reasons for this. First, many people contribute to design problems as I showed in *How Designers Think* (Lawson, 1997). Obviously they include the client, but they also include users, legislators and the designers themselves. Even more confusingly clients are seldom able to comprehensively state their problem at the outset. In fact clients are often still unable to clearly articulate the whole of the problem from their perspective even at the end of the process. Briefing is now generally regarded as a continuous process rather than one which takes place exclusively at the start of the project. The other contributors to design problems are even less likely to be able to give a comprehensive description of their aspects of the problem. Thus somewhat curiously design problems are most usually solved without ever having been completely stated. In fact today we consider that problem and solution emerge together but even at the end of a design process it is often the case that no one person or body is in possession of the whole problem description. This would by itself render the Alexander and Page views of designing impractical. It is probably fair then to say that it is often the case that knowledge about the problem and that which is needed to solve it is distributed among many participants. In this sense designing can seem a little like the process that fictional detectives go through in order to discover the identity of a murderer. Although many people in the story hold bits of knowledge none of them can put the whole story together. It is the special skill of the detective, who is also able to access all of the overlapping bits of knowledge, that yields a solution.

However, this argument must also mean that each designer or design team is likely to end up solving a different range of problems given the same starting point. We therefore must conclude that design problems depend to a significant extent upon the knowledge brought into the project by the designer. This feature of designing will turn out to be very important as we proceed through the arguments in this book. Zeisel (1984) argues that a characteristic of designing is that it works with two types of information which he calls a heuristic catalyst for imaging and a body of knowledge for testing. Essentially this tells us that designers rely on knowledge that helps them to decide how things might be, but also that they use knowledge which tells them how well things might work. The first kind of knowledge about how things might be is obviously prescriptive and not descriptive. Design is clearly a process that suggests how the world might be rather than one which describes how it is now. This knowledge is predictive but uncertain and laden with values. It is clear that the application of such knowledge is a highly selective process and therefore inevitably results in designers making their own unique interpretation of design problems. In theory Zeisel's second kind of knowledge, that is how well things work, could be more empirically based and more commonly shared. However, in practice the various fields of design have been relatively unconcerned with gathering post-project data in an organized and systematic way. There are some interesting arguments as to why this is, but it seems a major reason is the way in which design education traditionally fails to develop conventional research skills in its graduates. This of course is no accident, since the kinds of integrative, holistic and prescriptive thinking skills that design students need to acquire are of relatively little use to the researcher who generally needs to analyse, deconstruct and develop descriptions and explanations. This has recently given rise to problems over what exactly constitutes research in academic departments of design, but that is another argument (Lawson, 2002b).

Process sequence

This leads us on to the rather tricky question of the sequence of activities in the design process. Early work on the design process tended to suggest models that showed a progression from 'Briefing', through 'Analysis' and 'Synthesis' to 'Evaluation' and finally to 'Communication' (Fig. 2.4). A long time ago I argued that such models, although apparently logical, were not in fact supported by the evidence (Lawson, 1978). Sadly the RIBA in the UK still peddles this nonsense through its management handbooks and material for clients. However, more recently this basic idea has reappeared in a new form. Vinod Goel (1995) in a generally excellent book advances the idea that 'design

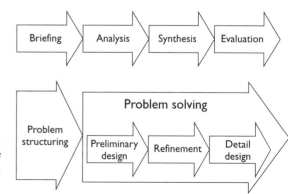

Figure 2.4
The RIBA and Goel models of
design as a sequence of activities

development occurs in distinct phases' This is in spite of the fact that his own data then shows that the phases he enumerates are not distinct at all. But Goel's phases are still of value to us if we drop the idea of them being either phases or distinct, but rather think of them as activities that designers do. Goel's activities are 'problem structuring' and 'problem solving', with the latter divided into 'preliminary design', 'refinement', and 'detailing'. It is true that all three of Goel's protocols show the designers beginning with 'problem structuring' and ending with 'detail design'. It is also true that in general the 'modal' activity passes through these four stages as the protocols proceed, but it is certainly not true that they are 'distinct'. Once we take other evidence into account about the design processes of experienced and outstanding designers we shall see that some at least use quite different sequences. An example of this is the outstanding Czech architect Eva Jiricna who is well known for her hi-tech interiors. Eva is quite explicit about regularly working from decisions about materials and detailed junction towards general arrangements (Lawson, 1994). Although an outstanding example, she is by no means unique and the American architect Robert Venturi expresses his sympathy for this approach with a typically wry aphorism (Lawson, 1994):

> We have a rule that says sometimes the detail wags the dog. You don't necessarily go from the general to the particular, but rather often you do detailing at the beginning very much to inform.

The components of design thought

This work then shows us that designing can be seen to comprise a number of mental activities. Clear evidence of this and of the way these activities are combined has tended to come most from what we might generally call protocol studies. These are examples of our second research methodology as outlined in Chapter 1. The designer is set to work under controlled conditions and is recorded usually using multiple media. The drawn outputs of the designer are kept and catalogued. Verbal outputs are usually created either by using teams of designers who naturally talk to each other, or by asking an individual designer to 'think aloud' while working. The whole is often video recorded so that actions and words are set into a single time sequence. The conditions usually include very limited access to knowledge outside, hardly any or no contact at all with a client or a potential user, and little or no interaction with other consultants, suppliers or legislators. In addition the whole thing is usually highly time constrained often being completed in minutes or at most one or two hours, and the designer has no breaks and is allowed no other activity.

Of course these controlled conditions are both the strength and weakness of this technique. In applauding its use a frequent employer of it observes (Gero *et al.*, 1998):

> There still remains a paucity of literature on how designers design which is based not on anecdotes or on personal introspection but on reproducible results, results which are capable of characterising designing.

The understandable attraction is that the results are *reproducible*, one of the key features of the natural science paradigm of research which has tended to dominate modern thinking. Indeed this is a very considerable attraction. However, the assumption that they are also 'capable of characterising designing' is far more questionable.

There are actually very real problems with such a technique. First, the reliance of the data on verbalization is dubious since it introduces a degree of introspection and conscious attention to process that is abnormal. We have shown evidence that suggests that the verbalization under such conditions may well not be a description of thinking that has just taken place but itself a director of thinking that takes place as a consequence (Lloyd *et al.*, 1996). Some researchers have used retrospective interviews in an attempt to eliminate some of these effects. Here the designer looks at the video later and at that time describes what thought processes were taking place. Of course this has the possibility of introducing other obvious potential distortions into the data. Designers are notoriously good at post-hoc rationalization of their processes!

Next the very restricted access to other sources of knowledge surely makes the designer almost entirely self-reliant in a way which may seriously distort the way knowledge is used in the designing process. The failure to allow for reflection and for time to pass, often while other tasks are performed, surely flies in the face of much anecdotal evidence on the way creative thinking takes place after periods of incubation (Boden, 1990).

For these two main reasons we must in this book treat this data with great care. However, there is a growing consensus from this kind of work about a number of features of designing that seem useful. There have been two main ways in which analysts have tried to break down a design protocol, which we might call temporal and relational. In the first case the protocol is simply divided into time slices. This seems to be useful when used at the macro-scale, perhaps comparing the first quarter with the last quarter to look for changes in styles or operations of thinking. Such divisions are rather crude and arbitrary and so other researchers have been tempted to reduce the scale of the temporal divisions. However, as the temporal slice becomes very small the arbitrary nature of it risks cutting across events that are clearly related. This suggests the second approach of dividing the protocol into events that seem to have some integrity, are related to each other and have some separation from other events. Clearly in turn this involves some interpretative skill and probably some subjectivity on the part of an assessor. But at the micro-scale it is probably the more sensible option, and it is work of that kind that we shall largely rely on to assemble our argument here.

Much of this work is essentially 'atomistic'. This is of course nowadays a rather misleading name since we now know the atom can be divided, but the description will suffice. In essence this work often concentrates on uncovering the smallest possible segment of a design protocol that it may be meaningful to examine. We shall consider those ideas here. Much of this research also then explores the relationships between these 'design process atoms' and compares what might happen early or late in the process or compares how experts and novices assemble these atoms differently. Some of this research, however, seems to lose sight of the distortions introduced by the conditions and attempts to generalize and infer in far too much detail about the overall nature of designing. Another problem with this kind of work is the way it tends to become self-reflective. As Gero and McNeill say in their own work (Gero *et al.*, 1998): 'Protocol data is very rich but unstructured. In order to obtain a detailed understanding of design processes it is necessary to project a framework on to the data.' Perhaps the most comprehensive attempt to deal with this problem can be found in a remarkable book that documents a conference held in Delft at which most of the world's leading practitioners of this kind of research all presented their analysis of the same two design protocols (Cross *et al.*, 1996). Many papers spend a great deal of time arguing about the relative merits of one projected framework against another. Perhaps it is in the very process of developing the framework that the greatest advance in thinking takes place. In arguing out these frameworks collectively we edge forward to some degree of consensus.

Design 'events'

So what are these smallest indivisible components of design processes? There is actually now considerable consensus at a fairly general level. Let us look for that consensus.

1. Design protocols can usefully be broken down into some segments that appear to be repeated not only inside one protocol but can be found in many protocols.
2. Judges can be trained to detect and identify these segments on a reasonably reliable basis.
3. There seems to be some hierarchical structure in which the smallest segments can be grouped together meaningfully into slightly larger structures.

What are these events? Clearly they may be physical actions, drawing, modelling, gesturing, acting. They might be verbalizations, especially when forced by protocol collection methods, or they might be entirely internalized mental operations. Such a breakdown does not seem to get us very far. Instead we might ask what intentions they reveal. Here we can say that they might at least include: a request for information, a structuring of a problem, a proposition about a possible solution characteristic, a representation of a solution characteristic, an evaluation of a solution characteristic. They may also include process intentions such as a reflection on the way the process is going, a decision to change direction, an evaluation of time or effort either past or future, and so on. This intent event as we might think of it might involve talking or drawing or moving or any combination of these.

Some writers refer to these events as 'moves', but that word is in fairly common parlance in design practice to describe a purely propositional action 'making a design move' as with the making of a move in chess. Others call them segments (Suwa *et al.*, 1998) but this does not seem to imply their 'atomistic' or indivisible nature adequately. Here we shall persist with describing them as 'events' and noting that there are many types of event.

Design 'episodes'

It is, however, clear from any realistic design protocol that events are usually not unconnected individual things. They are not 'units' or 'modules', but are often parts of some slightly bigger purpose. A group of such events may be seen as closely related to each other, carried out together in order to move the project forward in some way. It is also clear from design protocols that from time to time a new group of events begins. This seems to be for one of three major reasons. The existing task is either completed satisfactorily or has proved itself to be a dead end at least for now. A strategic event has happened causing a deliberate and contrived change of direction or emphasis. An outside event, such as a change of timetable, budget, or brief and so on, has occurred. Finally, and perhaps most intriguingly, a feature of the previous event has unexpectedly caused some new possibility to be envisaged. In Chapter 4 we shall see how the process of drawing can trigger this sort of change in thinking.

Some writers describe these groupings of events as 'chunks' or even 'dependency chunks', others as 'modules'. Here we shall simply describe them as 'episodes'. In a dramatic sense they consist of a series of transactions that deal with a particular theme or themes that can be used to punctuate a large narrative into the 'scenes' or 'acts' in plays and operas, or the 'chapters' in books, or the 'episodes' in longer running serials on television or radio. It is not the case that they are entirely discrete and separate from the rest of the narrative but that they seem reasonably self-contained.

The language of thought

That design is special has recently been recognized by cognitive science theorists. In particular the question that is asked by this area of study concerns whether or not we have a 'language of thought' and if so what is its nature? Since designers externalize so much thinking through drawing and in conversation it offers an interesting area to study. However, it turns out that understanding design in this way provides a challenge to the very core of the ideas behind modern cognitive science. Vinod Goel in his remarkable book *Sketches of Thought* (1995) explores this through a very sophisticated argument that is so grounded in modern cognitive science that it is rather inaccessible to those not fully conversant with his field. Nevertheless his arguments and supporting experiments are important to us here.

The essence of this complex argument is this. A computational theory of mind is predicated. That is to say we operate thinking through a language, if you like a 'language of thought'. This mental language, if it is to be understood through cognitive science, must have many of the properties of the natural languages with which we are familiar. Exactly why this step in the argument is valid is perhaps too detailed a matter for us in this book and readers who need convincing of this must brave the original text (Goel, 1995), or if they prefer an earlier and more general statement of the argument for a 'Language of Thought' proposed by Jerry Fodor (1975). However, common sense does not suggest anything different, for it surely seems a reasonable idea that we do indeed think in some sort of language and that this is closely related to the language we use to speak. Those who move to a foreign country often report that a significant step in their absorption of the necessary new language is when they begin to think and dream in it as opposed to their native language. Now while languages, even modern languages, vary they are all symbolic representational systems. Mathematics and many other human activities rely upon disciplined symbolic representational systems.

Design as problem solving

Cognitive science has cut its teeth so to speak on the study of problem solving. In the most general sense we can view problem solving as a very basic human activity and designing can be seen as a kind of problem solving. It involves a number of things. First, that the solver (designer) recognizes a state of affairs that needs improving and a target state of affairs that would represent the improvement. Next, for this to be a serious problem worthy of our study, we assume that it is not readily apparent how the solver (designer) can get from the unsatisfactory state to the improved state. This is all reasonably well understood and much explored by both cognitive psychology and more recently by cognitive science. Unfortunately both of these fields, and more particularly cognitive science, have tended to try to explain this process largely by reference to well-structured problems. Puzzles are excellent examples of such problems. Such problems can be extraordinarily complex, such as those found on a chess board, and so it has appeared as if this understanding applies to all instances of problem solving and thus to design. Sadly this is not so. Designers, as we are studying them in this book, solve not well-formulated problems but ones which are ill-structured, open ended and often referred to as 'wicked'. A more thorough exploration of the nature of design problems can be found in *How Designers Think* (Lawson, 1997), so that will not be repeated in its entirely here. However, for the purposes of this argument let us agree about some of the characteristics of design problems that make them special in relation to our concern. First, it is not clear that in the case of design problems the improved state can be undeniably and accurately identified. There may be an infinite number of states that offer some form of improvement over the current state and it may not be possible to entirely agree on their relative benefits. It is almost invariably the case that no one state can be thought of as optimal or the best state of improvement that is possible or even the best that has been discovered so far.

It is precisely the kind of mental activity that designers perform that challenges existing cognitive science. As Goel (1995) so worryingly puts it:

> as we move away from circumscribed puzzle-game domains, like cryptarithmetic, into more open-ended cognitive domains like planning, and design, and continue in the direction of the arts, cognitive science's ability to explain the relevant cognitive processes approaches zero. It is not that the problems are simply more difficult, so there is a steeper incline, and we simply have to work harder and longer; we seem to be facing a vertical wall, suggesting that perhaps something qualitatively very different is going on here.

The cryptarithmetic puzzles to which Goel refers are those where letters are substituted for numerals in a simple piece of arithmetic. A well-known example is SEND + MORE = MONEY. Solving such puzzles seems trivial by comparison with what goes on in our heads when we design, and yet explaining even this is a significant achievement for cognitive science. In this book we shall from time to time use examples of research done on chess players. While chess may be several orders of magnitude more complex than cryptarithmetic nevertheless it shares some features with it. The domain of operations is entirely prescribed and circumscribed. It is a board of eight by eight squares. A square may be empty or occupied by a single piece. There are exactly six different types of piece and the game always begins with the same known number of each type in exactly the same starting location. While there are a few variants such as 'en passent', 'queening pawns', 'castling' and so on, the moves allowed for each piece are otherwise rigorously constrained by predetermined rules.

Compare all this with design. Design has not normally got a predetermined domain. Sometimes in architecture or interior design there may be a site or space envelope but it is not divided up and remains an organic and fluid spatial limit. There are no predetermined pieces. Many things, in terms of functions, may occupy the same space and can usually take on an almost infinite range of configurations. In fact designing often begins without any clear statement of the problem as a whole. Some fairly general objectives may exist, but there is rarely an unambiguous way of knowing how well one is doing as one proceeds. Indeed design solutions are certainly not right or wrong as is the case with most puzzles. Even more confusingly, various solutions to a design situation may not even be capable of an overall assessment as to their relative value. Some may be better in one way while others may offer different advantages. So how do designers know when to finish their labours and how do they know which solution to select? That these simple questions cannot be given simple answers is what interests us here.

So the model of design as problem solving is clearly inadequate for our purposes here. Designing may involve periods of activity in which problems are solved and the process during those periods may indeed be problem solving. However, designing is sufficiently different from conventional problem solving, as we use that term in normal language, for us to need to investigate it further.

Designing then, in terms of chess, is rather like playing with a board that has no divisions into cells, has pieces that can be invented and redefined as the game proceeds and rules that can change their effects as moves are made. Even the object of the game is not defined at the outset and may change as the game wears on. Put like this it seems a ridiculous enterprise to contemplate the design process at all. To try to understand how it proceeds and what knowledge is used and develop some structure for that may seem foolhardy. But we shall try!

3

Sources and types of knowledge

We learn a lot from the client … we get some of our best ideas from clients, we love collaborating with them.

Denise Scott Brown

I describe this beautiful parrot sitting on my shoulder – multicoloured, very beautiful – called 'technology' … There's a little one on the other shoulder called 'art' or 'poetry', he's very powerful, squeaks a lot but he's not got the nerve of this one yet.

Ian Ritchie

Sources of design knowledge

Where does the authoritative knowledge that is used to make decisions during design originate? This probably seems to be a simpler question than in fact turns out to be the case. Knowledge that is used in the design process may originate from people and in places far removed from the current project. For example, at some point a designer may rely upon some theoretical knowledge that enables the sizing of a structural member in the solution. In architecture this might be the depth of a floor joist or a lintel over an opening in a wall. The knowledge that initially informed this may well have been collected and documented a considerable time ago and the theory formulated and expressed in many books, papers and other publications since. In many forms of design the solution may have to conform to some standards or legislative requirements. For example, the levels of electrical earthing or insulation in a domestic appliance such as a hair dryer. Here the standards may have been informed by empirical testing and then drawn up by other people who are unlikely have a direct connection with the current design project. An interesting question for us here is 'Who is responsible for bringing this knowledge to bear on this particular project?' Candidates for this would include the client, users, the designer and other members of the design team, legislators and those in positions of influence and power over what is eventually done. This structure reflects part of that which I used in *How Designers Think* when formulating a model of design problems (Lawson, 1997) (Fig. 3.1).

Goel (1995) argues from his analysis of a very limited set of experimentally gathered design protocols that, as they proceeded, the primary source of knowledge moved from being the design brief and the experimenter to being the subject or designer. As we saw in the previous chapter, Goel broke the design process down into a series of stages which he called 'problem structuring', 'preliminary design', 'refinement', and 'detail design'. We also saw that there is other evidence that challenges such a strongly linear model. However, what is interesting here about Goel's data is that the designer was the chief source of knowledge in all four of his stages. The designer was the source for about half the knowledge statements in the first stage and over 90 per cent in the subsequent three stages. This certainly strongly suggests that the vast majority of the knowledge used to solve the design problem was brought into the process by the designer.

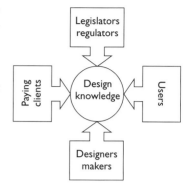

Figure 3.1
Sources of design knowledge constraints

Immediacy of knowledge in design

Unfortunately the designer in Goel's protocols was not provided with a context in which access to other sources of knowledge was either available or thought necessary. This is one of the serious failings of the 'laboratory' gathered design protocol upon which a great deal of our understanding is based. Perhaps this is also one of the failings of the studio system in design education. Most projects done by most students in most design subjects are completed with little or no real contact with an actual client, a potential user, a manufacturer or a legislative regulator. Some years ago my department was teaching design to students of architecture who, as usual in such situations, relied upon technical advice from lecturers in other departments such as Building Science or Structural Engineering. In fact the Department of Building Science shared accommodation with the Department of Architecture but the Department of Structural Engineering was in another building right across the campus. We had noticed that for some time we were frequently getting designs from our students that were innovative in terms of environmental design but very rarely so in terms of structural design where the work seemed much more conventional. We had wondered why this was so.

These students frequently complained that they could not get advice from the lecturers in Structural Engineering, so we investigated. The reality was that the structural engineering lecturers were very happy to give advice but used a somewhat cumbersome booking system which required the students to go and see a secretary who would then contact several lecturers and make an appointment with one of them for the student, usually within a few days. This it seemed had worked well for other university students but not the design students. When I challenged the architecture students about this they all came up with the same explanation. Once they had a design idea it seemed they wanted advice on it immediately. They simply could not progress their design process until this was available, and waiting even a couple of days they regarded as hopeless since they could not progress their work in the intervening period. As a result nearly all of them abandoned those ideas which required innovative or adventurous structures and developed other options using conventional structures about which they did not need advice.

A common topic of conversation among real designers centres on how frustrating it can be working with all the people who hold knowledge that they need access to. The inflexibility of the legislator who will not permit any novel variation from conventionally approved practice, or the lack of imagination of the client who cannot envisage a different approach. Other common examples include the caution of the supplier who will not contemplate an alternative material, or the quantity surveyor who cannot offer an opinion on costs without seeing a completed set of design drawings. All these are common stereotypes frequently heard in conversations between designers. The accuracy or otherwise of the stereotypes is not the issue here. The point is that since they so obviously exist and are so commonly talked about, they provide evidence of an experience of designing that reveals a heavy and central interaction with others and a critical and thus frustrating dependency on getting information from them.

The client and the brief

There are also other stereotypes that one commonly hears used in conversations between designers. It is quite normal for a designer to refer to 'having an excellent client for a particular project'. Even more directly relevant to our study is that designers also talk of getting 'good briefs'. Briefs are not it seems all of equal value, but rather some are better than others. Why is this? What can we learn from these ideas?

We conducted a survey of a sample of architects' views about their interaction with clients. The design practices surveyed ranged in size from a single person up to about 20 designers. The clients also ranged from single individuals who had never commissioned a designer before up to corporate clients who not only did so regularly but employed specialized personnel for this very purpose. This followed on from an in-depth set of interviews of both architects and more experienced clients. In the survey the sample size was 120 and the interviews were conducted on 12 architects and 10 clients (Lawson and Pilling, 1996). A further 11 famous architects have also been researched and interviewed about a wider set of issues concerning their processes (Lawson, 1994). The most striking outcome from all this data was the extent to which the experience of the client impacts on the nature of the design process.

The most common complaint from our survey was indeed about the nature of the design brief. When talking about novice clients it was common for the architects (54 per cent) to complain about the nature of the information they got in their briefs. This was backed up by several of the outstanding architects. For example, Eva Jiricna said (Lawson, 1994): 'We never, ever get a brief from the client which we can start working on.'

So what is wrong with these briefs? Interestingly it is often not that they are vague but that they are too specific. Several of our sample of distinguished architects made reference to wanting a very small brief to begin with rather than too much detail as Michael Wilford puts it (Lawson, 1994):

> What is an ideal brief for an architect or a design person? And we have found over the years that the ideal brief is probably one or two pages even for the most complex

project. Many clients think they've got to produce something which is two inches thick before an architect can even put pen to paper. We prefer it the other way round; we prefer the thinnest possible information.

Ken Yeang elaborated this idea by calling for a brief that 'only describes the objectives and is a sort of mission statement'. This was very much the result of our questionnaire. There was general agreement from over 83 per cent of the sample with the suggestion that the brief should concentrate on strategic requirements rather than be schedules of accommodation, and that any written brief at the outset of the project should be very short. However, there was also support for the idea that the brief was to be seen as a continuous process and indeed an integral part of the process of designing rather than some precursor to it. Richard Burton sums up this argument (Lawson, 1994):

> Briefing has become a much more sophisticated thing … than it was at one time and what is interesting is that the clients are beginning to understand that briefing is an absolutely crucial element. Now, what I don't know if they understand is that it's a continuous process, it doesn't stop and it's not like a kind of legal brief and that's it.

Legislators and the brief

Designers often find the legislation they have to work with very frustrating. This is not really because they would prefer not to have to respect the values that underpin the legislation but something to do with the way it is expressed. It is in fact very difficult to draw up legislation to regulate design. First, you have to embody all the values and requirements into a set of standards. Next, you have to imagine the way designs that must later satisfy these standards might be conceived. Finally, you have to set criteria and attach them to attributes of these as yet unimagined designs. This requires a huge amount of knowledge about design and the particular domain of design involved in order to make sense, achieve the objects and yet not unnecessarily restrict future designers. Sadly those who construct legislation rarely seem to have the demanding range of skills and knowledge that this requires. Later on of course the designer cannot discuss the legislation with the author and tease out any nuances or preconceptions which might just have crept in. This makes it particularly frustrating. The first set of British national building regulations was notorious for the range of buildings they unwittingly made illegal. For example, it was impossible, until they were rewritten, to design multi-storey car parks. Some might have thought this to be a major achievement but it was of course entirely unintentional. As a young architect working on hospitals that were exempted from the fire regulations (since one government department was not allowed to regulate another) I was able to design buildings that the fire officer at the time agreed with me were safer than they would have been had we respected the letter of the law in each case. I have argued elsewhere that legislation often focuses not on what is really desirable but what can easily be measured. It is often therefore framed in such a way as to encode knowledge in a form more likely to be helpful to the regulator than the designer (Lawson, 1975).

Users and the brief

Some years ago I was asked by one of the major brewery combines in the UK to help them develop better training for their designers. The organization was reliant for its business on a huge collection of English public houses. These pubs or inns were sometimes owned by the brewery and run by an appointed manager and sometimes owned by the publicans or 'landlords' themselves. Clearly the brewery had an interest in maximizing their sales of beer and to achieve this wanted to improve the quality of interiors in these pubs. However, it seemed that when a pub was refurbished the income was often not increased. There were actually several problems here. One was the rather ridiculous idea that the brewery had that it should use a national house style when in fact the evidence was that their patrons valued local differences. This was a problem of client briefing missing the point.

Another problem, however, was that of user briefing not being understood. It seemed that often the managers or landlords would report unwillingness on the part of the designers to listen to their advice. On the other hand the designers complained that they seldom got what they described as 'useful' knowledge from managers or landlords. Further investigation showed that actually the landlords and managers were characteristically very knowledgeable about what was successful or otherwise in a pub, but had no way of describing this knowledge to the designers. Such knowledge as they did communicate tended to describe solutions rather than problems. So they might tell the designers to decorate the pub with old horse brasses or use old timber beams and so on. The designers resented this, claiming it was their job to decide what forms and materials to use. Eventually we found a way of using techniques such semantic differentials to enable the landlords and managers to express ideas about the kinds of spatial qualities they thought would be successful and why (Lawson, 2001a). The semantic differential is most easily understood as a series of scales with opposite adjectives at either end of each scale. The respondent then selects points along the scales which feel right. The point about this technique that is of interest to us here is that it enables the client to express wishes about the kind of solution they would like but in a language that does not narrow down the choice of solution in ways that would restrict the creativity of the designer.

Clients and users, problems and solutions

The architect Ian Ritchie in conversation with me volunteered very similar notions when talking about the early stages of working with clients and how he tries to manage the knowledge transfer process (Lawson, 1994):

> The first move is to talk through the brief, understand what has led to it, understand fundamentally what it is about and that conversation is primarily about building up a level of confidence, of trust. That is the very first move and it's nothing about buildings, it's not about solutions or ideas about buildings.

All this evidence supports the notion that designers want the client to begin the process without preconceptions about the nature of the solution. This enables the process to begin with knowledge about human goals, strategies and desired behaviour. The designers responding here clearly see it as their responsibility to make the transformation into physical artefacts, components and systems. In fact it is also clear that they are telling us that they have special knowledge which enables them to do this which they do not expect to be apparent to the client. If the client, as so often seems the case with novice clients, tries to express the brief in terms of knowledge about the solution this actually has to be undone and the designer has to backtrack from this and transform the knowledge back into goals, objectives and behaviours. Eva Jiricna explains this (Lawson, 1994): 'Sometimes they [clients] have got totally rigid ideas what they want, but they are completely wrong from the conceptual point of view.' This was supported by another interview comment made by the same designer: 'If they [clients] start off with a written brief, it's only going to reflect what they already have.' This also hints at the idea that the client who expresses the brief in terms of solutions is more likely to do so in a conventional manner again preconceiving a design form which prevents the normal knowledge transformation of the design process. This is surely what Ian Ritchie meant when he said 'it's not about buildings'. Briefing it seems is a critical part of the process in which knowledge is introduced into the design and begins its transformation. To take this out, create artificial briefs and remove the interaction and relationships between the participants is to seriously change the design situation. The failure to recognize this is one of the most worrying aspects of much protocol-based design research. The architect Robin Nicholson echoes this quite explicitly (Lawson and Pilling, 1996): 'The briefing process is part of the design process.'

Establishing boundaries

Goel and Pirolli (1992) claim that designers also backtrack or 'reverse the direction of transformation' wilfully in order to engineer a problem that is amenable to solution by ideas they may already have. They cite evidence of designers in their protocols asking the experimenter (acting as a pseudo client) if they can enlarge the area of the problem they are responsible for. One subject reports an explanation of this by saying that: 'I'd come back to the client and say "well look, I really think that you should restructure actually the whole space, in between the building".' This also resonates with Eberhard's description of designers expanding problems through what he called 'escalation' and 'regression' (Eberhard, 1970). He amusingly illustrates the idea of escalation with a story of a designer commissioned to design a new doorknob for his client's office door. The designer begins by asking if he can consider the whole door, and pretty soon he is wanting to redesign the whole office! Those who have taught design students and set them studio projects will no doubt be very familiar with this kind of behaviour!

This example was deliberately chosen to be extreme; however, it serves to demonstrate an important characteristic of design knowledge. The designer in these cases is surely not being as cynical as Goel and Pirolli claim but is rather trying to define the boundaries of a problem which is otherwise indistinct. This may well be because the designer's prior knowledge of solutions suggests that a better overall result may be achievable by solutions to more widely defined problems. Many designers report a tendency of clients not to be able to see where the real possibilities lie when developing their brief, and thus designers may have a tendency to want to fully explore these issues for themselves.

An excellent example of this can be found in Richard MacCormac's description to me of the problems he encountered when designing a new set of buildings for a university. The university already owned a number of adjacent houses which were used for departmental accommodation and had asked MacCormac to add some further accommodation on what was a sensitive site in terms of conservation (Weston, 1990):

> The problem which the brief couldn't describe was really the problem of trying to attach new buildings to listed existing buildings in such a way that it would be acceptable to the conservation lobby, and would get planning consent, and yet would give a continuity of accommodation.

MacCormac eventually came up with a solution that involved building in the back gardens of these houses partially underground and thus adding new accommodation without really interfering with the original architecture. This solution had the added advantage of connecting all the houses without appearing to, allowing the departments in them to share new facilities and then to give the higher level organization of the faculty an architectural expression. In fact the solution was also able to distribute departmental common rooms in such a way that they could double up as expansion areas for the new lecture theatres. The whole result was a great deal less congested than would have been the case by sticking to the original schedules of accommodation. Both client and architect were happier with the final solution but as MacCormac notes it would not have been possible with the original brief:

> Now those issues don't appear in briefs often, they are the stuff of the thing which only comes out when you try and solve, when you try and produce a scheme and therefore the design process defines objectives in a way in which a brief could never do.

However, it is often not easy for clients to express briefs in this kind of way. A client formulating a brief has no theoretical mechanism for determining when the brief is complete. It often turns out to be the case that quite important things are not included simply because the process of assembling the brief did not trigger them as ideas for inclusion. Richard MacCormac expresses this in relation to design competitions where there is little or no interaction between client and designer:

> what's interesting is that often in competitions the winning scheme is one that tells the client something that they never knew before and that can be rather irritating because it's rather a hit and miss thing that often people win competitions because

they say something that the client suddenly realises is tremendously important to them and wasn't in the brief.

All this suggests that design takes place most easily, smoothly and probably successfully when the clients and designers are both able to express their own kinds of knowledge. The client knows most about the problems, needs and requirements. On the other hand designers tend to have considerable knowledge about design possibilities. Clients know what needs to be done. Designers know what can be done. In that knowledge of what can be done it seems that designers can also sometimes 'see' the possibility of solving problems that the client has not yet articulated but may be latent. In addition of course clients often have little or no knowledge of the other range of problems contributed by legislators and regulators whereas designers often have considerable experience of this area. Design then can be seen as a transformation between problem needs and requirements on the one hand and solution possibilities on the other (Fig. 3.2). Nigel Cross (2003) has shown that expert designers seem to have a particular way of making this transformation smoothly through a resolution of what might otherwise look like a conflict. We shall return to his interesting ideas on this in Chapter 5.

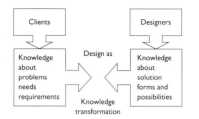

Figure 3.2
Design as a transformation between areas of knowledge

Importance and criticality

Lurking inside all this seems to be another issue which could be seen as the distinction between what is important and what is critical. A client may see some objectives in the brief as considerably more important than others. Indeed it is not unknown for a client to have only relatively few really important objectives in a brief that might none the less be very extensive. However, designers may not necessarily attend to those matters as much as clients expect since they may be perceived by the designer as not 'critical'. Critical constraints then are those that are most strategic in terms of the effect they have on the final form of the design and which most interact with other constraints, and which significantly impact on the range of options available.

One way of illustrating this is by yet again returning to Alexander's largely abandoned mathematical decomposition technique (Alexander, 1964). Chermayeff and Alexander (1963) used the technique in an otherwise very interesting book which attempted to show how to design housing. As the method required they first listed all the requirements they could think of. The method next demands that the positive and negative interactions between all the requirements are recorded. The method will then mathematically decompose the whole problem into clusters of requirements that have as little interaction with other clusters as possible. Among these were the following two examples:

1. 'Efficient parking for owners and visitors and adequate manoeuvre space', interacting with, 'separation of children and pets from vehicles'.
2. 'Stops against crawling and climbing insects, vermin, reptiles, birds and mammals', interacting with, 'filters against smells, viruses, bacteria, dirt. Screens against flying insects, wind-blown dust, litter, soot and garbage.'

Now any experienced architect will quickly recognize the first set of requirements is much more critical than the second. That is to say they have a far greater likelihood of making a significant impact on form. Probably you will want to think about them early on as they will have generative characteristics about large-scale organization and disposition of elements. The second set of requirements may have form-giving properties but in many cases can be solved merely through relatively minor technical provision in terms of the detailing of windows and doors. The Alexander technique was not able to exploit this knowledge since the computer performing the analysis did not have it. It is just the sort of thing that designers know.

These examples have been chosen for our argument here since they are fairly obvious. It seems likely, however, that the extent to which a set of brief requirements are critical is often not so obvious and certainly not obvious without considerable experience of designing and knowledge of design solutions that might be used in this case. A possible further complication here in the design process is that designers may choose not to reveal this criticality to their clients. This might be because they have not articulated it consciously to themselves, or because they judge that it may be difficult to explain. This may account for some of the many misunderstandings of the design process that arise among those only peripherally involved in it.

Direct lines of communication

Without experience as a designer, and in particular knowledge of a wide range of design solutions and their characteristics, it is difficult to understand what knowledge is important, when it is needed and why in the design process. In fact there is no theoretical way of knowing this. A piece of information may be critical and needed early in one design project since it has a strategic impact on the solution, but the same kind of information in another project may not. This will depend on all the other constraints which are at work in each case. Thus the idea that briefing is an early stage in the design process that consists of a one-way flow of information from client to designer, although persistent, is extremely misleading. In fact briefing is an integral part of designing and is more sensibly seen as a continuous and highly interactive way of eliciting knowledge.

For these reasons briefing is probably best managed by designers, either those working on the project or at least others having a real practising experience of designing. This could also account for the widely reported problems of using project managers in this role in design. I have lost count of the number of times designers have reported to me their frustration at only being able to communicate with their clients using formal channels controlled by project managers. In fact some years ago, within the space of one month, two different architects told me almost exactly the same story of such a frustration. In both cases they had felt the project was going badly and that they could not really get to understand the problem properly. One described the experience as like 'wandering around in thick fog trying to map out a piece of landscape'. Then quite by accident and totally unexpectedly they met their clients in a social context. In one case the architect and client got on so well they agreed to have dinner to discuss the project a few days later. Apparently at this point the 'fog lifted', the problems were more clearly understood and a direct channel of communication was opened up which persisted throughout the project. Both felt this event made a significant impact on the quality of the final design. In one case the architect and client remained friends socially after the project and expect to collaborate again but this time without a project manager for the design services phase of the work.

4

Drawings and types of design knowledge

A picture is something between a thing and a thought.
Arthur Symons, *Life of Blake*

'What is the use of a book' thought Alice, 'without pictures or conversations.'
Lewis Carroll, *Alice in Wonderland*

The drawing seems a useful source of potential insight into the knowledge that designers use. Designers are inextricably associated with drawings. When most people think of a designer they imagine someone who sits in a studio at a huge drawing board and above all else works with and through drawings. This image as we shall see is rather misleading, and actually designers draw in many places other than at drawing boards, and they also create physical models and computer models and representations. In fact they also talk a great deal among themselves and others. However, this must wait until later chapters. It is the drawing we are investigating here.

Design by drawing

We have not always designed by drawing. Originally, and still to this day in many places and under many circumstances, designers were and are primarily makers or crafters. They made objects ranging from small personal and household utensils, through larger pieces of equipment used in agriculture or other primitive industries, to houses and civic buildings and even complete towns. All this was largely made without significant use of drawn plans. Things were made by either copying or adapting what had been done before. This process is usually described as 'vernacular' when applied to architecture and as 'blacksmith' when applied to industrial products. The imaginer and the maker were parts of one single undifferentiated role.

Some charming documentations of such a process can be found in George Sturt's account of making cartwheels (Sturt, 1923) and of Benfield's account of stonemasonry (Benfield, 1940). A more thorough analysis of the characteristics of this primitive form of design is given in Chapter 2 of *How Designers Think* (Lawson, 1997). What is clear from such accounts is that the forms of knowledge used by the vernacular designer are quite different to those used by the modern professional designer. In particular vernacular designers clearly have a great deal of knowledge about the difficulties and practicalities of making and crafting their objects. In today's modern highly technical world with rapidly advancing and developing materials and manufacturing processes, the professional designer often cannot make the objects he or she designs. Such designers indeed may know surprisingly little about the making of their objects. However, the paradox is that the modern designer can adapt to new technologies and circumstances whereas the vernacular designer is hopelessly lost in the face of any rapid change. George Sturt's wheelwrights, for example, would have had no idea how to design wheels for a machine with an internal combustion engine or how to make use of the pneumatic tyre. The results of vernacular design are often attractive and may increasingly appeal to us in our uncertain and shifting modern world as they offer a glimpse of a more stable age. But the process of vernacular or craft design relying as it does on gradual adaptation is so unsuitable for our contemporary world that we shall not be much more concerned with it here.

The modern designer then experiments not with the object itself but with representations of it, and in this chapter we shall be concerned with the drawn representations. We shall examine them for the knowledge embodied in them and the insights they can give us into what designers know. The advent of design by drawing was to give the designer what Chris Jones (1966) so aptly described as a 'greater perceptual span'. The designer could experiment in the drawing rather than on the made object. The larger, more complex and expensive the made object, the greater the impact resulting from this change. It is not surprising therefore that architecture was transformed by this development. Of course in modern industrialized societies we now make even more expensive and complex objects such as aeroplanes, ships and spacecraft that could never have been contemplated without the power of design by drawing. In fact most of those objects would be hard to conceive of now without the next step forward of design by computer. We shall look at that in a later chapter.

Design representations

So important has drawing become in the design process that virtually every contemporary design curriculum places considerable emphasis on the acquisition of skills in drawing. Schools of design will generally go to considerable lengths to teach drawing methods and develop drawing skills in their students. This is usually thought so important and basic that it invariably starts right at the very beginning of the course. There are therefore now many good books to support these courses and among them a whole series by Tom Porter who has taught in schools of architecture for many years. In their primer on graphic techniques Tom Porter and Sue Goodman (1988) claim that 'in the wake of rapidly advancing computer-graphics technology, drawing by hand remains undisturbed as the central activity in the process of design'. Porter and Goodman's claim is certainly supported by the arguments in this book. Exploring designers' drawings is an excellent way to further our understanding of what designers know.

In terms of modern cognitive theory we must assume that there is some sort of correspondence between what is happening in the designer's mind and the representation that is made in the drawing. That representation may have a number of purposes as we shall see soon, but in each case it seems reasonable to suppose that it serves those purposes best the more closely the representation in the drawing matches the knowledge used by the designer. Thus drawings may be seen as a kind of window into the designer's mind and consequently into the designer's knowledge system and method of mental representation. It turns out that designer's drawings present cognitive theorists with a very considerable challenge in accounting for this connection between external representation and internal mental structure. In Chapter 2 we saw how contemporary cognitive science is turning to explore design and in particular how this attention is focused on the nature of design drawings.

Vinod Goel (1995) talked of meeting a 'vertical wall' when trying to understand design. It seems to be in the examination of the drawings that designers habitually do that we most obviously run into Goel's 'vertical wall'. The symbol systems used in these drawings are so open, variable, flexible and apparently indecipherable, and yet are clearly the very basis of thinking that they challenge the very idea of a symbolic language of thought as cognitive science can currently explain it. One of the problems facing us is that designers produce many different kinds of drawings for several different purposes. Each of these types of drawings has its own characteristics as well as purpose. Mostly when we look at them we can easily recognize the type of drawing in front of us, and yet just how we do this remains unclear. It would seem unlikely that we could write a computer program to perform this recognition task, never mind understanding the actual content of the drawing.

Types of drawings

Even a preliminary examination of designers' drawings will reveal that there are many different types of drawings involved. The first step in developing our understanding therefore must be to attempt some form of classification of designers' drawings. In fact Fraser and Henmi (1994) have already analysed specifically architectural drawings and suggested a classification system which offers a starting point. They identified five types of drawings which they called 'referential drawings', 'diagrams', 'design drawings', 'presentation drawings' and 'visionary drawings'. This is an interesting and useful taxonomy but one which is largely based on analysis of the characteristics of drawings. Here we need a slightly more elaborate taxonomy based on the way in which knowledge is being manipulated in the minds of the member of the design team and communicated to other participants. What is important here is that each of these kinds of drawings has its own set of rules. Such rules are clearly part of the knowledge that designers work with and yet they remain largely implicit. One of the problems with graphical communication is that unless the viewer knows how to interpret the drawing components, considerable misunderstanding can result. Because the knowledge about drawing types is largely implicit rather than explicitly discussed designers may easily fail to communicate knowledge to others as accurately as they think.

Of course some of these types of drawings may not be intended to communicate to others at all but rather to be part of the internal working of the designer or design team. These drawings are of considerable interest to us here. We shall therefore here investigate a range of types of drawings including presentation drawings, instruction drawings, consultation drawings, experiential drawings, diagrams, fabulous drawings, proposition drawings and calculation drawings. An added complexity here is that although these types have distinguishable characteristics any one drawing may contain features of more than one type.

Presentation drawings

These are the drawings through which designers communicate their work to clients and others from whom they may need some agreement, consent or permission to continue. They are characteristically intended to communicate decisions about the design to others who may have had no involvement at all in the design process. In some cases of course clients and users may have been involved to greater or lesser extents. However, the main purpose here is to convey information about the current state of the proposed design. This may be at what is expected to be the completion of the process or at some intermediate stage. Thus the drawings are primarily intended to explain what the final building or product would be like when it was completely made and in use.

Examination of such drawings and their use suggests that designers may have two possibly incompatible intentions here. They might at the same time perhaps wish to reveal and yet also conceal. They may wish to convince the viewer of such a drawing that the design is at least satisfactory or, more hopefully, excellent. The drawings presented in response to a design competition are most likely intended to impress, persuade and convince the jury. Drawings presented by architects to town planners in order to obtain planning approval might be expected to have similar objectives. We may assume that such drawings therefore are kinds of propaganda intended perhaps also to conceal weakness as much as to convey strengths in the design. For these reasons for the purposes of this book, these drawings are of least interest since, by the time they are produced, the design process is more or less complete, and because they may be the least reliably revealing of all the drawings produced.

Increasingly we are seeing that designers use computer techniques for producing these images. Such techniques, as we shall see in Chapter 6, often require a deliberate process of inputting information in a manner rather divorced from the process of thinking (Fig. 4.1). The example shown here in Fig. 4.1 is of a design proposal for a Hard Rock Café Hotel in Port Dickson in Malaysia by the architect Ken Yeang. The computer model rendering has been carefully calculated to communicate particular and selected kinds of knowledge while remaining mute about others.

Instruction drawings

These drawings are intended as an unambiguous one-way form of communication from designer or design team to constructor or supplier. They are usually

Figure 4.1
An architect's presentation drawing produced by computer. Ken Yeang's proposal for a Hard Rock Café Hotel in Port Dickson in Malaysia

only done after the designed object is largely resolved and they contain certain knowledge in the form of instructions for those responsible for physically creating the object. There are two variants. In some cases the drawing shows only the final form and constituent parts of the object while in others the drawing also shows the intermediate methods of construction. Examples of the latter might include those notoriously unhelpful drawings which accompany flat packed furniture from certain well-known retailers who prefer to leave their customers to perform the final construction. They serve to illustrate how difficult it might be to be entirely clear and unambiguous in instruction drawings. A common project in design schools to teach this skill is the submission of such drawings of simple objects to fellow students who must then perform the construction. The results are sometimes surprising to the author of the drawings. However, apart from this entertaining element of complexity such drawings seldom tell us much about the nature of design knowledge but rather about the nature of the finished article. The more common instruction drawings are those made for specialist expert contractors or manufacturers who can be assumed to understand a whole series of drawing conventions. The example shown here (Fig. 4.2) is again by the architect Ken Yeang. It shows two sections through a proposed building made to assist the major contractor. Again such drawings are deliberate and selective and tell us little about the nature of thinking that was involved in the design process. For this reason we shall not discuss instruction drawings much more here either.

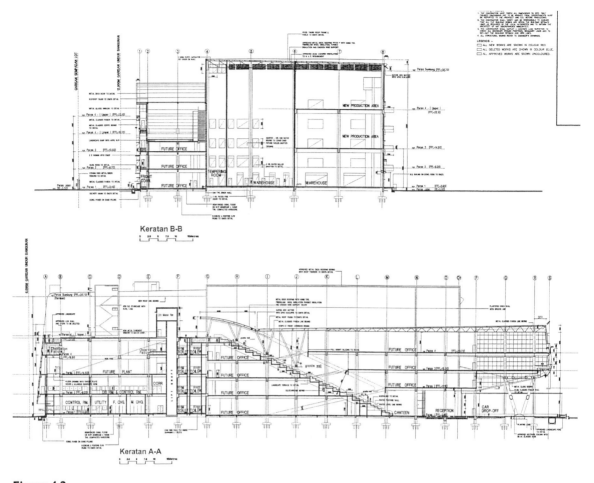

Figure 4.2
An architect's instruction drawing. A section by Ken Yeang

Consultation drawings

Consultation drawings could be thought of as a special category of presentation drawings in that they are primarily intended to convey information from designer to client or user or other participant in the design process. However, these drawings are done not so much to convince as to elicit a response in order to assist in the designing process itself. They may therefore be intended to lay out the bounds of knowledge and certainty about the state of the design so far. Often such drawings are done in preparation for a meeting to discuss progress. The Dutch architect Herman Hertzberger tells us that he likes to squeeze every available bit of information from this process. (Lawson, 1994):

> Clients always ask you to send a drawing one week before [a meeting] so they
> can study it, and I always try to find a pretext for not doing that, because I want to

present them myself and open the drawings and look at their eyes to see what their first reaction is and to try to detect what the hard points are, and then trying to listen to their first question.

There is a problem here of communicating uncertainty. Designers it seems need to be comfortable with the idea of differing levels of uncertainty within the design. At any one time they are likely to feel more confident about some aspects than others. Typically designers' drawings indicate uncertainty through style. A rough sketchy freehand style with a soft pencil is more likely to indicate the lack of definition compared with a more precise line drawn mechanically with a pen. Mark Gross (1994) quotes Anthony Pellechia from an MIT thesis in which he describes how Louis Kahn used very thick charcoal to sketch vaguely leaving his staff with problems of resolution:

> he cheated a lot. That charcoal line was very thick ... He would make everything work and then he'd go away. You wouldn't see him for maybe the next day, and you were left with these very thick lines that when reduced to realistic wall thicknesses and spaces – you couldn't put this functional stuff back in.

As Gross says designers tend to work with very thick and vague tools early in the process that make marks easily and quickly without too much precision or commitment and only later turn to a finer level of detail using pens and formal drafting techniques. How designers convey varying levels of uncertainty in one drawing, however, is less easy to see and it seems more likely to be done through a verbal commentary during a presentation. A problem here can be that a consultation is done which arrives at some form of approval based on a drawing that cannot easily be turned into a finer level of detail while still retaining the qualities of the vaguer consultative version.

A further possibility here is the presentation of two or more alternatives done deliberately to elicit a reaction from other participants that will help to arrive at a resolution. [Some designers seem to use a process based on this approach.] The architects Michael Wilford and Eva Jiricna, for example, deliberately use an alternatives generation design strategy. The drawings shown here are by Michael Wilford and show alternative basic arrangements for discussion with the client of Temasek Polytechnic in Singapore (Fig. 4.3). This development of alternatives does seem to be very much a matter of personal preference. Other designers, for example Richard MacCormac, clearly feel uncomfortable and prefer to elicit knowledge from the clients in a more abstract way, maintaining a single line of solution development in the mind of the client (Lawson, 1994).

Experiential drawings

Designers tend to draw habitually and certainly more often than just when designing. In fact many are excellent artists in their own right and most are prolific sketchers of the world around them. Why should this be? What clues does this give us about the nature of design knowledge? We shall see later that

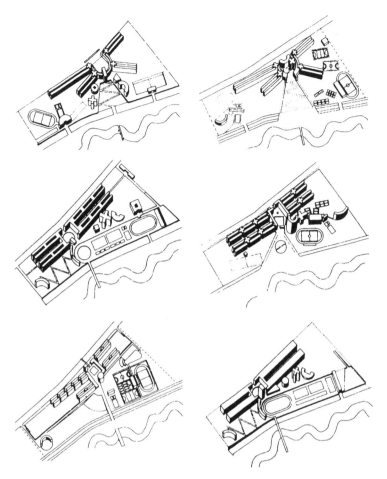

Figure 4.3
Consultation drawings of
alternative designs by James Stirling
and Michael Wilford for Temasek
Polytechnic in Singapore

this turns out to be a very important clue indeed about both what designers know and how they think. These experiential drawings are in fact part of the infrastructure of knowledge which every designer must establish. Herman Hertzberger describes this process in his excellent *Lessons for Students of Architecture* (1991) and we shall discuss this in more detail in a later chapter. The process of drawing is one of the best ways we know to absorb design ideas. The need to pass an idea from eye to mind and then to hand results in a level of understanding not necessarily achieved when simply looking at or even photographing an object or place. Perhaps this explains why so many designers keep sketch books to record things they see.

The English architect John Outram has a particular interest in both history and symbolism. His architecture is full of references to past architectural periods. More importantly he has a very elaborately constructed design process which relies upon building a symbolic language into his architecture. Outram, however, is not as precious about all this as might at first seem to be the case. He realizes that most people looking at his buildings will not be able to read them accurately as texts and this does not bother him (Lawson, 1994): It is sufficient for most people that they know there is a meaning, this enables them to engage with the architect at whatever level they choose. However, Outram himself is a considerable scholar and an avid recorder and analyser of architecture. His sketch books reveal not just a recording of buildings but are covered with analytical scribbles in his particular symbolic language (Fig. 4.4). Clearly although not done inside a particular project these experiential drawings form a vital part of the body of knowledge that Outram draws upon when designing.

We can see evidence of these experiential drawings emerging as part of a specific design process in the drawings done by Santiago Calatrava. The particular sequence here shows his reference back to the human form, a characteristic of Calatrava's approach, while working on the competition for the Cathedral of St John the Divine in New York. The sequence as shown (Fig. 4.5) is incomplete with many sketches omitted but we can see the diversion to redraw the human frame appears to have a strong organizing influence on the outcome of this particular design process. As with Outram, Calatrava is a prolific sketcher outside designing. His doctoral thesis was concerned with moving structures and he has developed a lifetime interest in these ideas. In particular he is a keen student of the human form and is fascinated by its ability to reconfigure in order to take on different patterns of loading.

There is some recent growth of concern in design education about the extent to which this sketching activity may be declining. The development of cheap photography made it easier to record experiential knowledge without the effort of sketching. Modern digital photography makes the recording of images virtually instantaneous and the storing of that material extremely cheap in digital media. The relatively recent advent of global image searching and retrieval on the Internet with engines such as Google may even reduce the incentive to make your own recording at all. The now commonplace use of CAD may mean that many young designers do far less physical drawing and may not be developing sketching skills. If all these factors conspire as they appear to be doing to reduce the ability and motivation of designers to sketch and make experiential drawings then future generations of designers may struggle to draw on experiential knowledge in ways, as we shall see later, that appear fundamental to the development of design knowledge. Only time will tell whether we should be concerned about this or not. Certainly Hertzberger makes a powerful and convincing argument of the need to pass the information through the eye–brain system in order to make the sketch. Without that mental effort simply seeing an object, building or place may have relatively little future value since recall may in turn be reliant on the media outside the brain. We shall return to this problem later.

Diagrams

Diagrams include all those drawings that we might normally describe as charts or graphs. They also include 'diagrammatic representations', or drawings which have so few of the physical or visual qualities of real objects that they cannot be considered pictorial. These are obviously 'thinking' drawings.

(a)

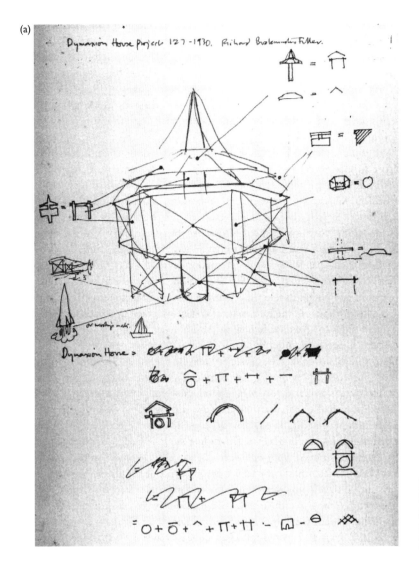

Figure 4.4
Experiential drawings by John Outram. Studies of Buckminister Fuller's Dymaxion House and Le Corbusier's Ronchamp Chapel

They are used to express some circumscribed characteristics of the objects being designed or the nature of the problems being solved so that they focus attention solely or chiefly on those characteristics. In essence then it is their very reductive or simplifying properties that distinguish them. They are deliberate attempts to remove information and to reduce complexity by setting up rules that automatically eliminate knowledge from the presentation. Such drawings seem to have two possible sets of content when used in design; they may be problem or solution focused. Perhaps the most well-known application of the diagram to design is the so-called 'bubble diagram', used by architects or planners when laying out the rough sizes and relationships of elements in the problem (Fig. 4.6). The drawing in this form is intended to show the important connections required between elements and is thus a graphical representation of what might be in a brief. Thus each bubble may represent a space and the

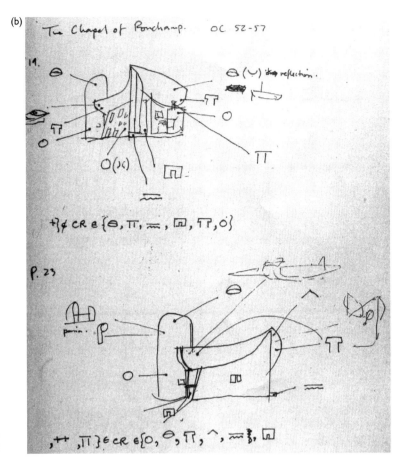

Figure 4.4
Continued

lines between them important circulation routes. The bubble is deliberately a rough shape intending to communicate that it does not represent the actual plan form of the space it stands for. Sometimes though bubbles may move slightly further towards the real object by representing the relative sizes of spaces in scale form. However, neither the shape nor location of the bubbles is to be trusted. This kind of drawing is in essence a topological graph. The famous London Underground map is another example showing as it does the connections between stations and the various tube lines that run between them. It does not, however, give an accurate indication of where a station is in London.

Such a drawing seems itself to be characteristic of the business of designing and gives a very good indication of the nature of design knowledge. Indeed the bubble diagram is an archetypal design diagram. It allows for some knowledge to be expressed precisely and unambiguously (relationships), includes other information which is obviously vague (size or location), and removes altogether all other information (for example, plan shape).

Diagrams are clearly therefore attractive to us when designing as they enable this temporarily restricted and simplified view of the situation allowing

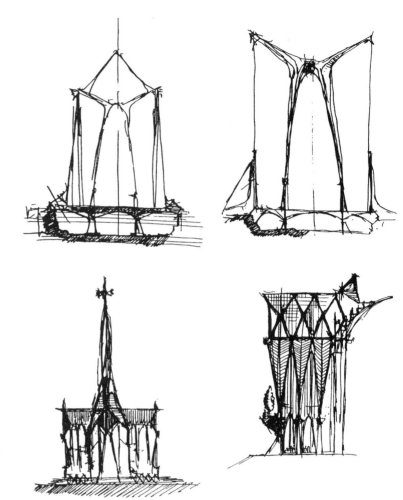

Figure 4.5
Experiential knowledge being used during design. Santiago Calatrava working on his competition proposal for the Cathedral of John the Divine in New York (sequence starts from top left hand corner and continues clockwise)

us to get our 'head around it' as it were. In my experience of teaching design they also carry with them many dangers. The diagram in fact only works if you play by the rules. As soon as you break those rules the drawing appears to be unambiguous on a matter that is actually rather uncertain, which is a most dangerous state of affairs. In a diagram, for example, the rules may be that the lines represent important movement of people between spaces and the boxes connected by these lines represent the spaces. If in some cases the lines between the boxes actually represent a desired visual connection or a strong service link and this different meaning is not articulated graphically then real confusion may arise. I have seen many cases over the years of students who have confused themselves with their own diagrams as they have begun to turn them into propositions and then referred back to them later without remembering this resulting in an unconscious overconstraining of a problem. Diagrammatic drawings which summarize some features of the design problem often thus take on the role of authoritative depository of that knowledge. Designers

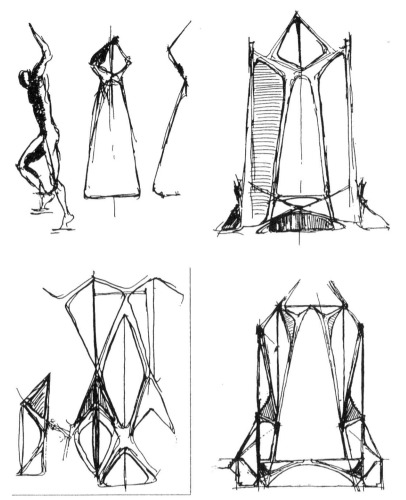

Figure 4.5
Continued

working in the face of enormous complexity complete such drawings almost in order to remove the responsibility on them to remember information. As we shall see very soon, the whole idea of many design drawings is to develop or evolve the solution. Such drawings are often modified many times over. There is therefore a great danger that this habit spreads to diagrammatic drawings which should have remained as fixed authoritative representations of knowledge rather than speculation.

Fabulous drawings

I have deliberately chosen the rather startling name of 'fabulous' to describe these highly speculative drawings. They are similar in nature to what Fraser and Henmi (1994) called 'visionary drawings'. Such drawings have many of the characteristics of both proposition drawings and presentation drawings. In many cases these also take on the appearance of art and may well be considered to be art in their own right. We shall here resist the temptation to debate what characteristics a drawing must have in order to be considered art. Indeed it may well be that whether a drawing is considered art or not cannot be discerned entirely from the drawing itself! Fabulous drawings are, however, quite commonly used by designers. They are 'fabulous' in the sense of having an intention behind them to express wonderful or fantastic qualities. These drawings are not used to test an idea but rather to let it flourish and develop so they are usually 'uncritical'. They are also 'fabulous' in the sense that monsters in the great fables were 'fabulous'. They often represent something that in fact could not exist. They thus suspend disbelief and criticism and realism. Such characteristics it seems are important in assisting the development of creative thought in some of its stages. The suspension of disbelief and criticism is of course one of the tricks practised in such creative thinking procedures as synectics (Gordon, 1961) or brainstorming (de Bono, 1970).

Piranesi is famous for his 'fabulous' drawings known as the Carceri. The spaces he portrayed were vast, impressive, daunting, vertiginous vaults which often distorted perspective rules and used every graphical technique to emphasize the labyrinthine qualities he was exploring. Lighting, tone and texture are all carefully exploited to leave the viewer with an overall impression of a place rather than an accurate representation of it.

Many famous designers are well known for their fabulous drawings. It is clear that the great German architect Hans Scharoun used such drawings and paintings quite normally in his processes (Jones, 1995). In particular Peter Blundell Jones in his authoritative book on Scharoun shows a series of sketches showing features of buildings that are suggestive of the ground-breaking design for the Berlin Philharmonie for which he is so well known. These sketches include features which are ambiguously neither clearly inside nor

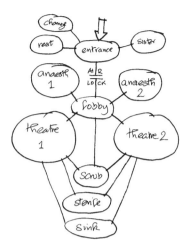

Figure 4.6
A diagram drawing showing a simple 'bubble' chart for the layout of a hospital operating theatre suite

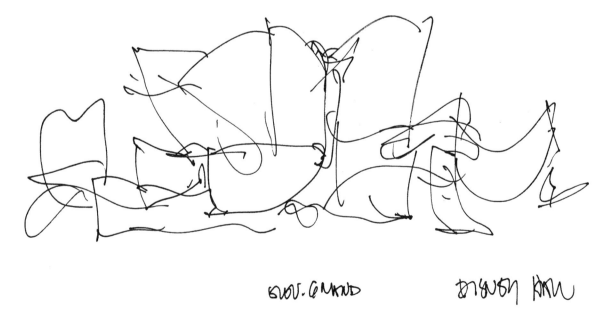

Figure 4.7
A 'fabulous' drawing by Frank Gehry of his Walt Disney Concert Hall in Los Angeles

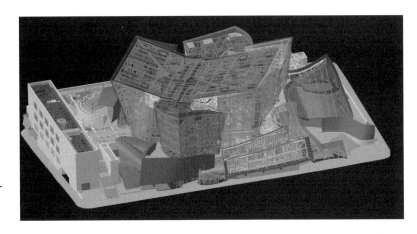

Figure 4.8
A later rendering from a computer model of the same building by Frank Gehry

outside the building envelope and yet others which clearly are one or the other. The whole is impossible to decode into a plausible space or physical geometry and yet wonderfully conjures up the qualities and ideas of his built projects.

The example shown here is by the architect Frank Gehry done while working on his design for the Walt Disney Concert Hall in Los Angeles (Fig. 4.7). Gehry is known for producing a remarkable series of buildings in the more recent part of his career that are almost 'fabulous' in themselves. However, this sketch can be contrasted with the computer model of the design (Fig. 4.8). We shall discuss Gehry's fascinating work again in Chapter 6 when exploring the nature of knowledge that designers share with computers. Here the sketch shows an almost uncanny way of expressing some of the qualities of this acclaimed and well-known building, and yet without in any way being specific about any particular part. The extent to which this knowledge is both vague and yet precise can be appreciated by the fact that many people, and certainly many architects, could recognize this sketch as being by Gehry and perhaps even tell which of his buildings it represents. Just as with Scharoun, Gehry is able very early in the process to express essential knowledge about a design that later turns out to be characteristic and yet which could have been interpreted in a whole multitude of ways.

Of course such drawings also carry great dangers for the designer too. Those who teach design will be very familiar with the student work that exploits such a drawing type perhaps deliberately in order to avoid the resolution of ideas into a working single whole. Powerful and imaginative but 'fabulous' drawings can be tools in the design process, but design is normally meant to come to a workable single end result and that definition cannot be expressed in the fabulous drawing however beautiful.

Proposition drawings

The proposition drawing is right at the very centre, the heart of the design process. These are drawings where a designer makes a 'move', or proposes a possible design outcome. Fraser and Henmi see them as so central to the process that they actually call them 'design drawings'. I am very reluctant to use that term as it suggests all the other drawings are not used in the process of designing. Of course they are but to varying degrees, which depend both on the nature of the design problem and the personal or team qualities, habits and preferences of those doing the designing. I have listed the various types of drawings so far roughly in ascending order of their apparent significance for the process of designing and of course proposition drawings come top of the list.

A proposition drawing more than any other must be of the kind that Donald Schön (1983) had in mind when he described the designer as 'having a conversation with the drawing'. The process here seems to be one in which the designer externalizes some features of the design situation in order to examine them in a more focused way. How that focus is organized we shall discuss in a later chapter. It is almost as if the designer were putting something down in order to 'stand back and look at it'. Designers describe this also as temporarily freezing something in order to explore the implications of it. The drawing then seems to 'talk back' to the designer and the conversation proceeds. We shall return to that in a little while. First, let us explore more of the nature and characteristics of proposition drawings and the kinds of knowledge they embody.

Some have argued that in general these drawings change as the design process proceeds from vague and sketchy to more precise. This can certainly be

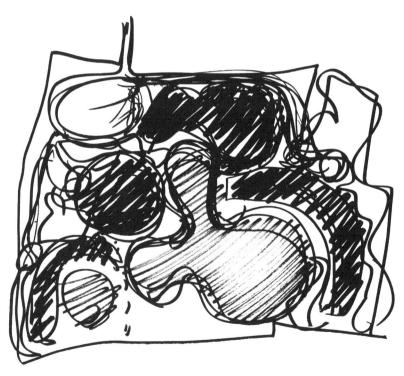

Figure 4.9
An early proposition drawing. Ken Yeang's plan for a Hard Rock Café Hotel in Malaysia

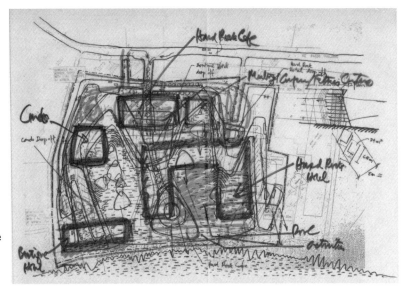

Figure 4.10
A further drawing done during the same project in which the architect is drawing over a more precise survey drawing of the site

seen in the sequence of drawings we see here done by the architect Ken Yeang again for a Hard Rock Café Hotel in Malaysia (Figs 4.9, 4.10, 4.11). Goel describing his experiments on the way designers use drawings argues this without entertaining any doubt about it. He tells us that 'there is an increase in the degree of explicitness and detailing'. However, these conclusions seem to be based on just two students who were doctoral graduates working under highly artificial laboratory conditions. In fact an analysis of the drawings done by experienced designers acting in the normal course of their profession may well cast considerable doubt on this simplification. My overwhelming feeling from conducting many investigations over many years is that 'laboratory' design processes are often quite different to those we see under 'real-world studio' conditions. In particular the extended reflection that seems to occur in the real world and which is actually facilitated by the designer doing other things over many hours, days, weeks, months and in some cases years results in far more iteration and a less clear directional pattern to designing. It may seem logical that designers go from the rough ready general considerations typified by sketches to the precise and detailed considerations typified by formal drafting. Indeed this may happen very frequently and it may be that it happens more often than not as a general rule. However, it is certainly clear that a significant number of highly proficient and reputable designers may not only work to some extent from the detailed to the general, but can and do articulate this and that this can be substantiated by examining their drawings. The architect Eva Jiricna, for example, has said (Lawson, 1994):

> In our office we usually start with full size details … if we have, for example, some ideas of what we are going to create with different junctions, then we can create a layout which would be good because certain materials only join in a certain way comfortably.

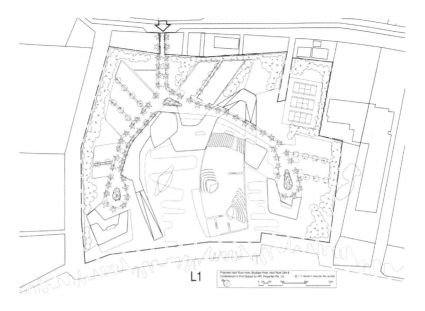

Figure 4.11
A more firm and resolved version of the plan

This is a design process based upon working from the idea of a selection of materials, through an understanding of how to join them, to detailing where there are junctions and from this creating a vocabulary from which the overall arrangement is constructed. This is certainly not the general to the specific and appears to be almost the opposite. The evidence of Eva's drawings supports her description. The American architect Robert Venturi combines both directions in his process and although perhaps less extreme than Jiricna is equally articulate about this (Lawson, 1994):

> We have a rule that says sometimes the detail wags the dog. You don't necessarily go from the general to the particular, but rather often you do detailing at the beginning very much to inform.

These architects may be dismissed as eccentric exceptions to the rule, but actually it is not hard to find many other examples of design processes that work from particular to general. The English architect John Outram combines both heavily symbolic architecture and a love of the technical in his highly individual process. Outram could be seen to work from both the general and the particular. His explanation of his process shows an extraordinarily wide sweep of ideas about the site and its history about which he writes his own mythical description. At the same time there is a very particular construction of what he has actually referred to as new 'orders' of architecture. His shows very considerable similarities to Jiricna's approach by first establishing from the technical detail a design lexicon from which to construct the wider plans.

A particular example of the detail as generator of idea can be found in the wonderful example of the Italian architect Carlo Scarpa. Scarpa worked on the Castelvecchio Museum in Verona over a period of several years based in the building itself designing and drawing as construction work proceeded. This extraordinary process has been lovingly and meticulously documented by Richard Murphy (1990) who points to the intertwining of making and design through the process of detailing that seems so characteristic of Scarpa's approach:

> Designing, detailing, discovering, building, testing, discussing: for Scarpa these must all be simultaneous activities. Without such a climate to facilitate this way of working, his method and his work would never have been possible.

In a separate study Steven Groak (1992) recounted that Scarpa himself described how he implemented this process by drawing. Unfortunately we no longer have Scarpa's original proposition drawings but before Groak sadly died suddenly and at a cruelly young age he was able to assure me of the validity of this reconstruction. Scarpa was working on the handrail detail for a wooden bridge in the Castelvecchio (Fig. 4.12). In this design the handrail is narrower than the posts which support the balustrade. Groak was sure that Scarpa had wanted the handrail to be 'graspable' by the average hand but knew that he needed thicker uprights for structural strength. Scarpa was working on the detailed junction of these two elements and drew a proposition that the upright would be cut down to the handrail width some small way below but far enough to allow a hand to run along grasping the handrail without interruption by the vertical supports:

> In drawing the lines to show where the cut edges would be, he encountered the familiar problem of the draughtsman: how do the lines cross? Do they overlap? Or stop at a point? Scarpa realised that the carpenter would face an analogous problem in cutting the piece of timber (although in fact it is not a complicated task for a skilled craftsman). Eventually he decided that the carpenter should drill a small hole at the intersection of the lines, so that the saw would change tone when it then hit the void and produce a clean cut with no overrun. To complete the detail, he then designed it to have a small brass disk inserted in the circular notch left behind.

This wonderful example of a series of proposition drawings encapsulates beautifully the idea of the drawing talking back in the conversation. They also illustrate yet another example of a designer who characteristically worked up from detail.

Calculation drawings

This type of drawing can perhaps be seen as a special case of proposition drawings. They are drawings that are effectively made as an alternative to doing some calculations. How high will a roof reach if it is at 30 degrees over this building? What distance will the staircase travel to reach from one floor to the next? How large would a radius of an arc be that connected these two lines?

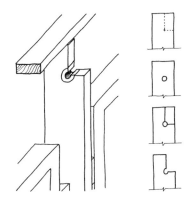

Figure 4.12
A conversation with the drawing. Carlo Scarpa (Stephen Groak's recollection taken from *How Designers Think*)

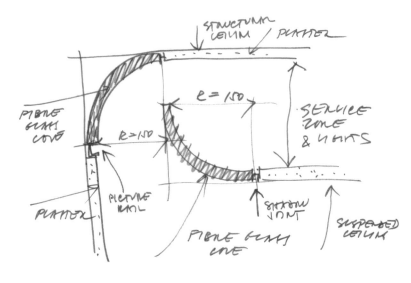

Figure 4.13
A calculation drawing. Eva Jiricna
calculating the size of a ceiling
coving detail

Would there be room to get a car through this gap? How many cars can we park in the basement of the building? Such examples explain a drawing which is performed in order to see how some aspect of a proposition will turn out. They are not done for visual effect or to communicate to others but merely to work out the implications of some state of a design proposition. Sometimes calculation drawings are fairly rough and at other times they may be quite precisely constructed using formal drafting methods or CAD. The example shown here (Fig. 4.13) is by the architect Eva Jiricna working on a conversion of a private apartment. She has already decided to use a suspended ceiling and is exploring the detail of how the ceiling will meet the wall. She is calculating here the radius of the coving that will produce the effect she wants to see.

Types of drawings

So what lessons can we draw from all these examples? First, as our general experience tells us, designers make extensive use of drawings and they are often central to the thought processes employed. We can see that designers use drawings not just inside a project but as a way of storing knowledge and linking ideas from one project to another. Experiential drawings in particular are obviously created for this very purpose. Again our general experience tells us that designers are usually very visual people. Not only is it their business to produce things we primarily experience visually but the common image of a designer is one who may dress differently and be very conscious of visual style in terms of their possessions and interests. However, the analysis in this chapter also confirms our view that the visual world which designers seem to understand and appreciate is actually one which they manipulate directly. Most of us are so used to manipulating thought through conventional language that this may seem a little strange. Mathematicians it seems can manipulate their own symbol systems directly as can musicians who do not need to translate the marks on a musical score into a conventional language but can go straight to the sound patterns. So it seems designers are able in some way to think visually. In the next chapter we shall explore the idea that much design knowledge may be visual in form.

5

Manipulating design knowledge embedded in drawings

I want to see therefore I draw.

Carlo Scarpa

I could take a big piece of paper and draw the whole thing, but I prefer to concentrate.

Santiago Calatrava

In Chapter 2 we investigated some aspects of the special nature of design that makes it so interesting to study. One of the features identified, which has particular significance for the arguments in this chapter, is how design is characteristically holistic. A single feature of a good design solution can simultaneously solve many aspects of the problem. Design solutions and problems do not map onto each other in predictable or theoretically describable ways. This means that designers cannot really break down problems in the way classical natural science researchers do. Designers have no way of knowing in advance which aspects of the problem can be integrated into which solution ideas. For this reason the designer seems to have a special way of thinking which is integrative. In fact the predominant style of thinking that design students tend to develop during their courses is one in which they drag issues into a debate and widen the terms of reference rather than one in which they focus and analyse. Of course this is cognitively extremely demanding, since it seems everything must be thought about at once. This means keeping in mind, as it were, many disparate factors, which on the face of it have little or no relation to each other. While they may not appear to be related in the problem, eventually they may be solved by the same idea in the solution. So how do designers perform this mental juggling act?

The evidence suggests that the drawing acts as a kind of external memory in this regard. Putting something down on paper is always a useful way of remembering that you have to do something. The ubiquitous 'to-do' lists of modern time management software are a powerful testimony to that. For the designer it seems likely that drawings offer a more graphical version of this aide-mémoire facility. While exploring a complex set of issues for which there are no logical or theoretically correct subdivisions, the drawing can act as a way of 'freezing' some features for a while as others are explored. The propositional drawing is also the designer's way of making, recording and testing hypotheses. The propositional sketch becomes a sort of graphical 'what if' tool.

An architect trying to organize the plan of a complex building might draw one or two spaces that are required to be very directly linked thus creating a larger clump the configuration of which might for a while act as such a design hypothesis. Such a drawing is acting as a way of saying 'What if we fix these spaces like this?'

So what are the characteristics of drawings that might do this job well? Several features seem to be highly desirable to make a propositional drawing contribute usefully to design thinking. We must remember that at this stage the designer may not have a complete solution and may know very little about the rest of the solution configuration or characteristics. For this reason the drawing should only show what is temporarily fixed and highlight what is being investigated. The drawing should not suggest that the design currently answers questions which are not yet being addressed, and should not imply that more is known about the solution than is really the case. Similarly the whole style of the drawing should indicate the level of precision or resolution which the designer feels at the time of making the drawing. So we have two requirements here: one about content and one about style. It sounds pretty tricky to achieve, but in reality designers do this all the time, if only one can 'read' the drawings they make accurately. They seem to achieve this partly through training and partly by repeated and extensive practice. However, it is clear that designers choose the type and content of their drawings with these factors in mind. They also choose the style of their drawings to match their level of certainty and commitment to the ideas being expressed.

When I interviewed leading designers about their processes many of them wanted a piece of paper in front of them before they would begin the conversation, or would break off in order to fetch one if it was not there to begin with. Many designers report feeling almost unable to think without a pencil or pen in their hands. When I interviewed John Outram he left the room to bring in a sort of pencil tin in which there were many felt tipped pens, crayons and other similar media. He was able to select from this tin as the conversation proceeded and he made his points. He could select big rough pens and smaller more precise ones. Richard MacCormac discussed this habit in considerable detail and talked of his 'thinking pencil' (Lawson, 1994) and of how he needs to use different drawing instruments to mediate different modes of thinking at various stages in the design process:

> These different frames of mind involve different instruments for producing and representing what you are doing ... whenever we have a design session or crit review in the office I cannot say anything until I've got a pencil in my hand.

The dependency on the drawing instrument and the need actually to hold it while thinking seems very real. Thus even one of our most talented and sensitive architects can say that 'I haven't got an imagination that can tell me what I've got without drawing it.' (MacCormac in Lawson, 1994) Even the acclaimed Italian architect Carlo Scarpa admits something similar (Murphy, 1990): 'I want to see things. I don't trust anything else. I place things in front of me on the paper so that I can see them. I want to see therefore I draw.'

The drawings done by Robert Venturi for the extension to the National Gallery in London illustrate the development of design ideas through drawing in a particularly interesting and revealing way (Fig. 5.1). This very high profile scheme was already very complex before Venturi, Scott Brown were taken on as designers. The site is in Trafalgar Square, one of the world's great urban spaces. The new Sainsbury Wing had a major donor who was effectively a second client. The original design by Ahrends Koralek and Burton, which had won a high profile competition, was criticized very publicly and notoriously by Prince Charles. The new American architects must have felt the eyes of the world were watching over their shoulders as they drew! In addition to the normal requirements of the art gallery this extension had to relate to the spatial organization of the existing Wilkins National Gallery with its raised ground floor axial planning, and had to provide a major new entrance and yet still give public domain pedestrian access from Trafalgar Square up to Leicester Square. All in all, a pretty demanding set of constraints.

Venturi's propositional design sketches show some interesting characteristics. In particular they illustrate not one line of thought but at least two. These 'parallel lines of thought' have been identified and analysed elsewhere (Lawson, 1993). In this case one line of thought appears to be a consideration of the building as a sequence of spaces which are explored mainly through plans. What is apparent here is the way one drawing leads on to another in the sequence. It is also clear, particularly in the earlier steps, that thinking is developing even within each drawing with many lines overlaid on each other (later drawings in the sequence can be seen in Figs 6.4 and 6.5 in Chapter 6). The other line of thought seems to be concerned with the resolution of the urban context and is developed mainly through elevations (Fig. 5.2).

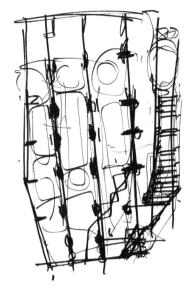

Figure 5.1
A proposition drawing by Robert Venturi for the National Gallery Extension in London. It clearly reveals a line of thought about the building as a sequence of spaces

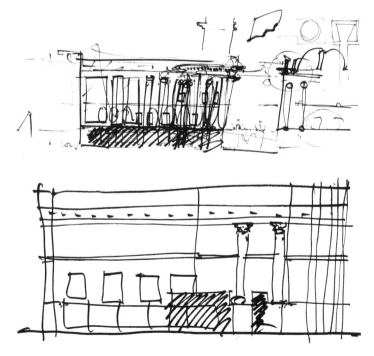

Figure 5.2
Another drawing for the same project as Fig. 5.1 but this time showing a line of thought about the building as urban elevation

In Venturi's early sketches in the plan sequence we can see that he is drawing space rather than envelope. There is little evidence of him considering the materiality or structure of the building. By contrast what seems to be in his mind is the sequence of spaces that a visitor to the gallery will pass through and walk around. Many lines are drawn over several times and in some drawings this reconsideration is very significant. This represents an excellent example of what Donald Schön (1984) has memorably described as the architect 'having a conversation with his drawing'. Venturi's partner Denise Scott Brown has her own way of describing this when she talks of 'Bob having a facility between hand and mind ... sometimes the hand does something that the eye re-interprets and you get an idea from it' (Lawson, 1994). It is certainly apparent here that the drawing is playing a very central role in Venturi's design process and that the act of drawing is integral to his thinking.

Size of drawing

Much design research, as we have seen, involves pseudo-laboratory conditions. Under these circumstances designers are often not working in the conditions and with the materials they would choose for normal practice. If we study the actual drawings that real practising designers create when they are working we find some interesting and frequently repeated patterns and characteristics. One such characteristic involves the size of drawings done by experienced and distinguished designers, and in particular concerns their propositional drawings.

In my study of the design processes of outstanding designers over half of them volunteered information about their preference to use relatively small drawings (Lawson, 1994). Fraser and Henmi (1994) analysed the drawings of Le Corbusier, who sketched prolifically, recording things that he saw as a huge 'experiential' drawing database. The vast majority of these drawings were less than A4 in size. The question here is whether there is any important reason other than simple convenience for these small drawings. Michael Wilford, who has not only been very successful in his own name and was for many years the partner of James Stirling, prefers to use either A3 or A4 paper and is quite explicit about this as an office policy (Lawson, 1994):

> I like to see things encapsulated in one small image. We have a rule never to draw at a size larger than necessary to convey the level of information intended ... we always use the smallest possible image.

Indeed many of the drawings I saw on the projects Wilford was working on were actually A4 in size even for huge projects such as Temasek Polytechnic in Singapore, a colossal higher education campus. Similarly the great Spanish architect/engineer Santiago Calatrava generally works on very small drawings for his large airports, railway stations and even cathedrals. For small drawings to be used on such a big scheme suggests even more firmly the significance of this. In fact Calatrava seems to work with several media in parallel. He works freehand in watercolour on an A3 pad, and has generally A5 spiral bound notebooks in which he sketches with a drawing pen. Again Calatrava is quite

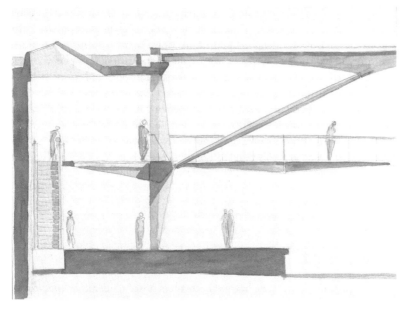

explicit about this (Fig. 5.3): 'I could take a big piece of paper and draw the whole thing, but I prefer to concentrate.'

The highly influential Dutch architect Herman Hertzberger (1991) used a very similar phrase to Calatrava in referring to his preference for working in A3 sketchpads: 'I insist upon having my concentration on quite a small area.' In fact Hertzberger went on to explain this in even more explicit terms and the explanation seems to offer the possibility of a more generic reason for this popularity of small drawings among designers: 'It's a sort of imperative for me, you know … like a chess player. I could not imagine playing chess in an open space with big chequers.'

As it happens, just around the corner form Hertzberger's office in Amsterdam I found a large open air chess board on which some locals were playing. This surely must have been in his mind when he made these comments. Playing in public is surely a bad enough torment for most of us but there is yet another problem with such huge chess boards. They are so large that you simply cannot 'take them in' all at one glance. To see the whole board clearly you must at least move your eyes to scan it or more likely move your head or even walk around. This is because the field of human vision is not regular. Only the central part of the retina, known as the fovea, affords really clear and focused sight, while the peripheral parts of the retina specialize in detecting motion. Such a system is quite understandable from an evolutionary point of view, but may be less well adapted to large-scale chess playing.

For most of us the fovea is such that we can see clearly the whole of an A4 sheet of paper when held at the distance from the eye normally used for drawing. When Calatrava and Hertzberger talk of 'concentration' this surely is what they mean. The designer can see the whole thing at this size and concentrate on all the contents of the drawing without losing sight of any elements. Any larger and this particular quality of experience disappears.

Bearing in mind what we discussed in Chapter 2 about the special features of design this perhaps becomes more significant than it might at first seem. The holistic nature of design means that often a single design feature simultaneously solves many parts of the problem. Designers clearly know and understand this and the need to manufacture an integrative response places on them this burden of keeping many things in mind at one time. Having the whole drawing in clear foveal vision would seem a very sensible pattern of behaviour under these circumstances. However, once we study the nature of expertise in design rather more closely in a later chapter yet another reason for this behaviour for using small drawings will become apparent.

The dangers of drawings

Of course the 'greater perceptual span' of design by drawing as opposed to vernacular design enabled greater rates of experimentation and therefore increased the risk of failure. The more we innovate from one design to another the less reliable will be the designer's knowledge of 'what might work'. But there is another great problem with the process of design by drawing. The drawing is of course merely one form of representation of some features of the object that are not yet made. Every form of representation has its own characteristics and therefore strengths and weaknesses in representing imagined objects and conjuring up in our minds the experience of those objects in real use. The drawn image has conventions of views but all those conventions are essentially variations on a theme of geometrical and spatial relations of one sort or another. In other words the drawing is good at representing how the object will appear to the eye and how the various constituent parts of it are related in space. While this may in itself be valuable knowledge it is far from being a complete and comprehensive representation of the features of many commonly designed objects which really matter to their eventual users.

Selectivity of drawings

The Malaysian architect Jimmy Lim asked a conference of architects recently if when they get home in the evening the first thing they do is to take their favourite armchair across the street and sit down to admire their house. The question of course was rhetorical, and unsurprisingly not even one architect present admitted to this somewhat eccentric behaviour. 'Why then', he continued, 'do you all spend so much time drawing the elevations of houses you are designing.' His point of course was that the experience that matters to the users of a house is far more to do with the interior space than the front elevation. Now it just so happens that Jimmy is a master of tropical domestic interior space so we might imagine he has a vested interest in making this point. However, the generic lesson is well made, which is that drawn representations themselves distort and change the emphasis of our experience much more profoundly than we realize. The drawing conventions of elevation and plan so common in architecture can neither ever actually be seen nor experienced.

They are the designer's version of political spin. We see what they for some reason wish us to see. Of course the more serious danger here is that designers come to work not on the real object but on the drawn image of that object as they design. Anyone with any experience of teaching design students will recognize such a danger all too readily. We shall return to this problem of the knowledge embodied in drawings later.

The drawing is somehow so powerful a tool that it can easily become an end in itself. In *How Designers Think*, I identified a series of common traps which inexperienced designers commonly fall into (Lawson, 1997). One of these was called the 'image trap' in which the designer ends up designing the drawing rather than the object the drawing represents. Herman Hertzberger echoed this concern about the role of the drawing and its potential to become the focus of attention rather than a representation of knowledge about an emerging design (Lawson, 1994):

> A very crucial question is whether the pencil works after the brain or before. In fact what should be is that you have an idea, you think and then you score by means of words or drawing what you think. But it could also be the other way round that while drawing, your pencil, your hand is finding something, but I think that's a dangerous way. It's good for an artist but it's nonsense for an architect.

The drawing can also restrict rather than enhance the designer's vision of the problem. In a very early but highly significant study, Eastman (1970) demonstrated this effect empirically. He had asked his subjects to design a bathroom. Eastman records how the kinds of drawings used by his subjects during the experiment actually affected the problems they discovered and solved:

> The accessibility to children of sink fixture controls becomes an issue only with the generation of a section representation ... Generally, a clear correspondence was found between the kinds of constraints that could be considered and the representations used.

Drawings as symbol systems

Goel (1995) arguing from a cognitive science perspective sees design as a manipulation of representations which he analyses as symbol systems. He notes that both the brief and the final production drawings are representations. Several points about this are interesting to us here. First, the brief is usually, but not as exclusively as Goel seems to think, a textual representation. That is to say it is largely a matter of written sentences, notes, lists and so on. The production drawing is largely a pictorial representation, though again not exclusively since it usually contains many notes and textual labels which are often essential in making it comprehensible. It is often accompanied by almost entirely textual specification documents. Overall, however, Goel's point is a very sound one. There is a very substantial shift from verbal to graphical information representation during design. However, there is another difference between these two representations in that the brief (and we are making huge generalizations here) is largely a set of human requirements, goals, aspirations and desired behaviour. By comparison the production drawing is a depiction of physical components, their interconnections and information about how to construct them. As Goel observes, designers progress from the first representation to the last through a series of other representations largely transforming one set of knowledge into another. This fact while being stunningly obvious nevertheless remains a central and most interesting one to us here.

Rather remarkably designers do not traditionally provide any information to their clients about the transformation. One can look long and hard at a set of architectural production drawings and the full written specification which combine together to make the contract documents. Nevertheless no amount of looking will reveal any substantial connections with the briefing document if there was one. Somehow the client is expected to work out whether the brief is satisfied by the design and if so how well and by what devices. On the face of it this does not seem much of a service that the architect has delivered. As we shall see when we explore computers and design knowledge there may be ways of improving this service. However, it remains central to us here that designers can somehow transform one set of knowledge about people, behaviour and goals into another set of knowledge about artefacts, connections, structure and physical properties.

We might then ask if cognitive science can help us to understand this transformation since it offers the possibility of a rigorous and coherent analysis of how symbol systems work. Unfortunately as Goel so eloquently demonstrates, it is not really able to do this. In fact an analysis of the symbol systems of the various types of drawings we have discussed already here is not really possible. The main reason for this seems to be that the work which is done on symbol systems is chiefly concerned with the relationships between symbols rather than what they represent. For our purposes this is not particularly helpful. This is something that is rather too often forgotten by design researchers who assume that to transform design drawings into a limited mathematical notation system is somehow to make progress. What it might do is to enable a logical sequence of arguments but it is unlikely to shed any real light on the nature of the knowledge embodied in those drawings.

Drawings as transformations between problem and solution

However, all is not lost since other research may help us here. Nigel Cross (2003) gives a fascinating insight into how this might happen, at least for designers with high levels of expertise. Cross makes three case studies from different data but all concerning accounts of how highly regarded industrial designers achieve a resolution of conflict in a particular design project. In each of these three examples the designer appears to find a way of relating problems and solutions by framing the problem in such a way that some fundamental principles can be brought to bear in order to remove conflict. One of Cross's case studies is of the highly successful racing car designer Gordon Murray. Enthusiasts of Formula 1 racing will remember the 1981 season when the authorities banned the use of 'ground effect' designs. This technique had combined very low clearance cars with smooth under-bodies and flexible side skirts to create a ground gripping force enabling greater traction. But the authorities had been concerned about safety and in 1981 introduced a regulation requiring a larger minimum ground clearance in order effectively to eliminate the use of the effect. Cross reports how Murray 'saw' the problem as a conflict between requiring the ground effect and the new regulations apparently denying it. He then employed the basic principle of the down-force effect that could be achieved from the airflow over the car body at speed. This led to the use of hydraulic suspension systems which effectively lowered the car while racing but returned it to an acceptable height when parked and measured for clearance. This represents an extraordinary piece of highly successful ingenuity.

In all three of the Cross case studies this pattern of conflict resolution between the designer's description of the problem and the client's wishes about the final solution could be observed. In one case, that of Kenneth Grange, the fundamental principles used to resolve the conflict appear to be highly personal rather than a piece of theoretical physics as in Gordon Murray's case. These personal values and ideas seem remarkably similar to the idea of 'guiding principles' that I have already described elsewhere (Lawson, 1997) and which we shall explore again in a later chapter in this book. These insights from Cross, however, show that expert designers can find a way of transforming problems and solutions so they can be connected through some principle order to remove conflict.

Further evidence to support this idea comes from the interviews I have conducted with a number of highly successful architects already referred to here (Lawson, 1994). The Dutch architect Herman Hertzberger indicates that although his process generally moves from brief to solution he almost 'sees' solution form in the brief itself:

> I am not starting with the form, I start with organising the brief, to make the brief for the design and then, the funny thing with my brain is that when I start to formulate the conditions and organise the things in the brief then the form comes up in my mind.

This is echoed by Richard MacCormac:

> A sense I have is that architecture is a kind of analogical or metaphorical way of thinking and I think architects try and translate the stuff of briefs into some kind of structure as soon as possible.

What this argument hints at is that transforming knowledge about the goals and behaviour of people into knowledge about the structure and relationships of artefacts is difficult precisely because the two systems of knowledge cannot be mapped directly onto each other. Clearly this requires considerable experience and expertise and we shall discuss the nature of design expertise more fully in a later chapter. This also relates to our realization in Chapter 2 that design is often an integrative process, that is to say some parts of the solution may solve many parts of the problem. Our task here then is to understand how designers make this remarkable transformation through the representations that they use in conversations, written text, drawings, physical models and computer models.

What do designers 'see' when they look at their drawings?

Suwa and Tversky (1997) have studied the way designers use drawings in design protocols and what they see in them. They suggest that designers attend to the very figural or formal properties of sketches as they make them and from this tend to 'read off' new ideas about function. This very strongly parallels Goel's argument that there is something about the nature of sketches that promotes this transformation. As Suwa and Tversky put it the sketch becomes a 'perceptual interface' between form and function. This also has some similarities with what Schön and Wiggins (1992) describe as 'unexpected discovery' from looking at design sketches. Suwa *et al.* (1998), also analysing design protocols, suggest that the frequency of what they call 'functional actions' tends to increase immediately after a period of what they describe as 'spatial arrangement'. From this they infer that sketches are 'providers of visuo-spatial clues for association of functional issues'.

To some extent this begs a very important question that we can only answer more fully in a later chapter. The question is 'To what extent can designers perceive ideas about function from the forms of their drawings because of something to do with the drawings themselves or something to do with knowledge they already possess?' As we shall see later the answer is almost certainly both. However, for now we shall concentrate on the nature of the drawings.

The symbolic and formal content of design drawings

We know from a very influential early experiment by Bartlett that we have a tendency to remember drawings not in terms of their iconic or formal organization but in terms of their meaning or symbolic representational value (Bartlett, 1932). Bartlett famously ran an experiment in which he showed subjects a drawing which they were asked to remember and to return later to his laboratory and reproduce from memory. Bartlett would then show this drawing to another subject and repeat the procedure and so on through perhaps a dozen or so iterations. In one startling experiment Bartlett showed how a conventionalized Egyptian owl or mulak, always ended up as a black cat at the end of his sequences. In a sequence published by Bartlett the tail of the cat could be seen to appear both to the left and to the right of the animal. Similarly details such as collars and whiskers appeared, disappeared and reappeared in the sequence. Bartlett concluded that subjects were not relying on a memory of the shapes, lines and patterns in the drawing but on the ideas that the drawing represented. This enabled subjects to reproduce details that had not been in the original drawing but also to omit details that had. Of course a subject who had no knowledge whatever of cats and of our conventionalized way of drawing them would not operate in this way but instead have to rely on memory of the pattern of lines and shapes. The fact that Bartlett's sequence began with a conventionalized drawing of which his British subjects had no knowledge, however, reinforces his conclusion. These subjects it seems were more likely to see the drawing as cat-like thus relying on symbolic memory rather than remembering the lines and shapes which would have required them to rely on iconic memory.

One of my research students, Alexandre Menezes, has developed this idea to further investigate what designers see in drawings. He showed two drawings to his subjects, one an abstract image by Paul Klee, the other a plan design sketch by Mies van der Rohe. However, Menezes' subjects were asked to describe these drawings to another subject who had to reproduce them from the description without being able to ask any questions. The subjects were from two groups of students of architects. The first group had only just begun their studies and the second were post-graduate students with at least five years of experience of study and practice in architecture.

The description protocols obtained from this experiment are amenable to similar subdivision into chunks or sequences that develop a description by what Goel (1995) referred to as lateral and vertical transformation. That is to say a particular part or relationship of parts in the drawing is described in a variety of ways each related to the previous one (lateral), before a deliberate change to a different aspect of the drawing (vertical). This mirrors results of previous studies of what designers perceive in their design sketches (Suwa and Tversky, 1997).

The more experienced design students described both art sketch and design drawing in a shorter time than the novices. However, in this shorter time they managed to pack in more ways of describing the same image. They also described the design drawing more quickly than the art sketch and character-ized it as 'easier' to describe. The novices on the other hand thought the art sketch was easier to describe. Preliminary detailed analysis shows that the more experienced design students tend to use symbolic references to design precedent whereas the novices use formal geometric descriptions more. It seems that symbolic descriptions such as 'it looks like a squashed sun' are more economic in time than formal geometric descriptions such as 'it is a long flat ellipse with some lines growing radially from it all round and extending out about as far as the vertical diameter'. Although the art sketch was capable of symbolic descriptions, these are entirely metaphorical. Clearly the experienced designers recognize precedents more readily in their home context. Put simply, designers are recognizing architectural or design ideas for which they have schemata to which are attached symbolic descriptions. Provided the recipient of the information knows these schemata the symbolic descriptions are very compact compared with the formal or geometrical characteristics. To see how this works imagine saying 'tartan grid' compared with trying to describe such a formation through geometrical formal properties.

All this suggests that if we wish to understand the drawings that designers do when they are working on a project, we need information beyond those drawings in order to interpret them. Quite simply they cannot be viewed as self-contained symbol systems. They are likely to make reference to material in ways which are so ambiguous that no automated system of analysis could possibly understand. Effectively then you must know what was in the designer's mind in order to read the drawing. This helps to explain why Goel was absolutely right to raise his concerns about the value of current cognitive science in trying to understand design. We shall return to this in our final chapter. It also raises several profound problems for us. It makes the use of design drawings as a tool for understanding design protocols very difficult and inappropriate as a technique by itself without other supporting evidence. It also suggests that there may be potentially huge problems when design drawings are looked at by other people with different backgrounds such as clients or potential users. Even more difficult then is the idea that drawings might be exchanged usefully and meaningfully between designers and computers. That is the subject of our next chapter.

6

Exchanging design knowledge with computers

Asking 'can a machine design?' is similar to asking 'Can a machine think?'
Nigel Cross (2001)

the internal representations of most CAD programs are not amenable to abstraction or ambiguity.
Mark Gross, 'The electric cocktail napkin' (1996)

This is not really a chapter about computer-aided design and most certainly not one about computers. There are many other books about both. The reader interested in CAD and in particular the intersection between computers and architecture would do well to refer to any of the interesting series of books by William Mitchell (1979; 1990; 1995; 1999). This chapter is about what designers know as revealed to us by this relatively recent encounter with the computer and even more recently with the Internet. Both have the potential to revolutionize designing in the way that drawing did. In fact so far the computer has not done that and the lessons from this are ones we shall examine here. Actually a very great deal of what is described as computer-aided design is in reality computer-aided drawing and is therefore of interest to us here in a similar way that manual drawing is. In fact computer-aided design has turned out to be rather a disappointment so far. There is little evidence that it has significantly improved the quality of design or made designing a better experience. As Nigel Cross (2001) so succinctly puts it: 'Why isn't using a CAD system a more enjoyable, and perhaps, also a more intellectually demanding experience than it has turned out to be?' Cross argues that using CAD may in some cases be quicker but is more stressful and that there is no evidence that the results are better. Could it be possible that this has to do with the way computers and human designers manipulate knowledge? If so some study of CAD, its achievements and deficiencies may tell us quite a bit about what designers know.

The roles of the computer

Computers can actually play several quite different roles in the design process and it is around these roles that we shall base the start of our exploration here.

It is interesting that the earliest attempts to use computers in the design process were actually very much more ambitious than we would even contemplate today. Not surprisingly their success was very limited as we shall see for reasons we now understand. Perhaps the biggest disappointment in this field is the still rather limited success in getting computers actually to assist in the real business of design as opposed to performing relatively menial supporting tasks.

The history of technology is one of the amplification of human capabilities. Mechanical devices have amplified our strength to lift and move objects including ourselves. Optical devices have amplified our ability to see either further as with the telescope or in more detail as with the microscope. Biotechnology has amplified our control over nature in order to feed or heal ourselves. Computing technology has amplified our cognitive abilities to store and recall information and to process it more speedily. This is certainly true for computer-aided drawing. We can now store and manipulate graphical information in the design drawing office at rates that were unimaginable only a couple of decades ago.

The other great potential the computer has appeared to offer us is the ability to support our cognitive and creative processes. However, by comparison the potential of the computer to aid creative thought in design has proved more difficult to realize and remains a largely ephemeral mirage (Lawson, 2002a). Many claims have been made by the industry for software that was then only used for relatively short periods of time by enthusiasts. Why is this? What can we learn from it about the nature of design knowledge?

The computer as 'oracle'

The first serious attempts at computer-aided design positioned the computer as 'oracle' or font of wisdom. In this role the computer actually produces a design proposition. An early example would be a program to design single storey building layouts by optimizing circulation patterns (Whitehead and Eldars, 1964). Boyd Auger's program for designing housing layouts maximizing sunlight, view and privacy offers another such example (Auger, 1972). Strathclyde University's programs designed layouts for schools given a timetable of classes. These programs actually proposed designs with the human designer relegated to the support role of resolving, tidying and rationalizing after the computer had proposed the main ideas.

The assumption was that somehow the computer designed propositions would be arrived at more quickly, with less effort and be more optimal than those achieved by human designers. When this was investigated by Nigel Cross (1977) he found that while on average the Whitehead and Eldars program was indeed slightly better at optimizing circulation than human designers, the best architect beat the computer. It is probably the case that today we might have even better algorithms for such problems so if the program were to be rewritten now it is possible that it might be better than the best architect just as the latest chess playing programs can now beat grand masters.

More recently this role has had a reprise with other kinds of programs that also design in extremely limited ways. Many researchers have published proto-software of this kind based on the idea of geometrical rules such as shape grammars (Mitchell, 1979). In such software the computer uses rules which are either implicit or sometimes explicit in existing designs to produce new variants based upon these organizational constraints.

John Frazer has for many years worked with a set of ideas which involve computers generating families of solutions from such sets of rules. In the early days this required the designer to give the computer some limited piece of form as a sort of 'conceptual seed'. The computer would then 'cultivate' this seed through standard transformations such as stretching, rotating and the like. These 'mutations' of the original idea could then be presented back to the designer as a sort of source book of ideas. More recently the biological analogy in this process has been extended to include the idea of 'evolution' (Frazer, 1995). In a whole series of demonstrations, Frazer and his team have now shown how computer programs can be developed with what he describes as 'genetic' algorithms.

Architectural concepts are expressed as generative rules so that their evolution can be accelerated and tested. The rules are described in a genetic language which produces a code-script of instructions for form generation. Computer models are then evaluated on the basis of their performance in a simulated environment. Very large numbers of evolutionary steps can be generated in a short space of time, and the emergent forms are often unexpected. Here the computer is designing in a way which is in theory predictable but in practice may be quite unexpected and thus apparently creative. Even the author of the program who may have some rough idea what it will do may still be surprised by it in much the same way we may be surprised by another human member of a design team. At the moment these ideas are really research tools and whether they will progress into tools used as part of an everyday design process remains uncertain. However, so far there is little sign of any widespread use of such ideas for actually designing.

So why is it with all the power of modern computers and the sophistication of contemporary computer science we see almost no use of computers in this 'oracle' role in the design fields studied in this book? There may be several reasons, but one stands out in terms of our analysis so far and adds supporting evidence to the understanding we are building up of what designers know. By now perhaps the reader can already see the parallel here with what was discussed in Chapter 2. The computer as oracle is a high technology replay of the early design methodology approach exemplified by the failures of the methods proposed separately by Christopher Alexander and John Page. What use is a computer designed building that only optimizes circulation, privacy or view? We have seen that the nature of design solutions is that they are frequently holistic responses that are integrative. You are most unlikely to arrive at them by first producing a series of sub-optimized solutions?

We could conceive of a suite of programs each optimizing buildings against individual criteria such as energy consumption, circulation, construction costs, lighting and so on. In such a scenario the human designer might be presented with the outputs from each program but this is unlikely to be helpful since the task of reconciling all these alternatives is no less challenging than the original design task. Designers it seems reject this idea because they know it is unlikely to move things forward in a constructive way that would help their process. The problem here is that so far we know of no way to make these programs communicate usefully since we have no rational way of trading off all the variables against each other.

So this idea of the computer as 'oracle' or font of wisdom has so far proved to be something of a mirage. In fact this is by far the most ambitious of all the roles that computers have been forecast to play in design. If we examine this role in terms of its fundamental characteristics then one argument would suggest we shall never be able to realize this vision of a computer actually designing. Design of the kind we have been studying in this book could be seen as one of the most intellectually demanding types of thinking. It involves both procedural and declarative knowledge. It relies heavily on experience and common sense. These are issues that we shall explore more thoroughly in the following chapters. The idea that a computer could be programmed to perform this range of cognitive tasks has been promoted by the field of Artificial Intelligence. In essence this field takes the position that given enough capacity and power, computers simply by manipulating symbolic representations of knowledge, could effectively 'think'. But we have seen that the sibling of AI, Cognitive Science, has struggled to represent design knowledge in this kind of purely symbolic manner. Some have argued for many years that AI is in fact a mirage and that human thought must involve much more than simply the logical manipulation of symbol systems. Probably the most developed and sustained argument on this front has been advanced by Dreyfus (1992).

This book will not reprise that argument in detail but the analysis of design knowledge presented so far here and as it will be further developed in the remaining chapters, gives strong support to the idea that computers as we know them at present are not capable of becoming useful partners as designers. Persisting with attempts to get them to support designers is, however, an enterprise that offers much more immediate promise. We shall therefore examine a number of less ambitious roles for computers in design to see what further we can learn about design knowledge.

The computer as draftsman

We are by now all familiar with the computer as 'draftsman'. It almost seems that once we discovered the computer could draw we have become mesmerized by this capability. Perhaps we still admire computer graphics in almost the same way we are amused by animals trained to perform human-like tricks. However, if we return to the analysis of the roles of drawings developed in the previous chapter we can see that perhaps all this is not quite so clever. In fact computer-aided drafting is now commonplace in many design fields and most certainly in architecture, though it is really at the stage of production or presentation drawings that the existing technology comes into its own.

When a drawing is developed over time and has to be edited and altered perhaps by many people then computer drawing systems have many advantages. They separate out the process of creating the information from that of reproduction or printing. This is both de-stressing for the composer of the drawing and enabling in the sense that many different kinds of reproductions and scales can be used from the same data. These systems enable repetition, transformation and other powerful timesaving devices. They allow for consistency and quality control. In fact they enable the management of information in so many ways that they have distinct advantages over purely manual drawing techniques. However, these advantages largely become apparent not at the designing stage, but at the later presentation and instruction drawing stage.

There are in fact more problems that trying to work with computers have thrown up from which we can learn lessons about what designers know and how they think. These problems concern what knowledge is in the computer and what in the mind of the designer. They also concern how that knowledge is communicated between these two powerful partners of human and machine.

Pixels versus components

Let us imagine we wish to enable a designer to draw on a computer screen or on a digitizing tablet. We have several levels of problem to address before this process will begin to resemble more conventional drawing. The first level is the ergonomic level. The mouse has the disadvantage of not actually being at the point where a mark is being made, whereas the pen on a tablet or touch sensitive screen is. This distinction may not matter too much in the creation of a mechanical drawing but the mouse or trackball is generally reported by designers as too remote. They simply cannot control the mark being made anywhere near directly enough to feel what they are doing. The pen still does not actually make the mark but simply conveys information to the computer which in turn draws the mark on the screen (and later perhaps prints or plots it). Again designers report this as too remote for, it seems, three commonly reported reasons. First, there is no friction between pen and screen so they get no 'feedback' from the movement. Second, the mark made does not respond to pressure or speed of movement in a predictable and expressive way. Third, an interaction between the first two problems is that the designer gets no feedback feeling from variations in pressure and speed of movement.

However, we are not really concerned with such ergonomic problems here and many more intractable difficulties begin to emerge once we try to make connections between the knowledge the designer is using and the data stored in the computer. How are we going to store in the computer the mark the designer has made when drawing? There are really two options each with a number of variants but really only two basic principles. These two options are reflected by two kinds of graphical software that we have become familiar with. The first is the sketching software that we might find on a palm pen interface computer or in the very simple programs supplied with Macs and PCs. These are basically pixilation devices. We are used to our television screen and now our digital camera operating on this principle. Basically the graphical area is divided into many tiny dots or pixels. As the pen moves across the screen or tablet those pixels which it crosses are triggered and illuminate resulting in a line that approximates to the line drawn. Draw with a thick pen and the result will be several pixels wide, while a very thin pen may only manage to trigger a path one pixel wide. This is fine so long as all you want to do with the image is store it and reproduce it. You might even send it through some editing software to give it better contrast or change the colours. But basically you have not interrogated the collection of pixels and inferred anything from them.

The second kind of software is that we see in more traditional CAD packages. These are basically vectoring devices. To get a straight line you simply indicate either end. The computer will store these two points and some information about how thick and in what colour you want the line. When the computer comes to display this on a screen or plot it the software then calculates how to draw the line. This is simple enough of course, and such systems usually have another element that allows you to draw any number of consecutive lines as if in a graph, or even to create a closed polygon. But such an approach does not stop with the straight line. It can include arcs or circles, for example. Usually to draw a circle in such systems you indicate the centre and anywhere on the circumference. Perhaps we might get clever and draw an arc which is a partial circle so now you need to point to each end and the centre. Of course we can get even cleverer and include B-splines and all sorts of free but rational curves. The fact is all these are simply elements that can be rationally described to a system which has a mathematical representation of them and can thus reproduce them as desired.

Now the problem for us here is this. What is in the mind of the designer when sketching? Is it more likely to be something like pixels or something like the graphical components of drafting systems? There is simply no evidence to believe that our knowledge is pixelated and common sense and everyday experience would suggest that it is not. However, our knowledge may well be much more fluid than the rigid language of a CAD system graphical component library. But our lack of shared knowledge with the computer runs far deeper than this distinction between pixelated or component-based knowledge.

I am designing a building, let us say a small house. I have never seen this building in real life because it does not yet exist though I have seen many that resemble bits of it in some way or other. I do not, however, yet really know how it all fits together and there are many parts, aspects and qualities of it I am very unsure or totally ignorant of. And I start to draw it. Moreover I imagine myself standing at some point near the building looking at it and I work out how it would look as projected onto a flat screen in the form of perspective. Actually of course the drawing itself helps me to this. I am quite likely to choose to start with a major feature, perhaps the outline of the main walls. Once I have done this I can now see where to make the marks for the roof in relation to the walls. Then I can see easily how to locate and represent detail such as windows and doors. This is one of the ways designers converse with their drawings. This surely tells us that a designer knows, as he or she is drawing, something about what the marks in the drawing represent. Even the sequence of drawing these marks is likely to be informed by this knowledge. Put simply I am likely to draw walls before the windows in them and so on. We shall return to that problem in due course, for now let us just consider the drawing itself as opposed to what it might represent.

So I come to work at a computer and in addition to advancing my own thinking, I must stop and work out how to make each mark on the screen.

This is usually a multi-step process, let us remember. First, work out which graphical element in the system you are going to use. Then select it from a menu. Then remember the sequence of inputs for that element and make all the appropriate pointing and clicking movements. This is no longer a conversation; it is a halting clumsy process that more closely resembles the assembly of a sentence in a foreign language with the aid of a dictionary.

So quite simply the designer must have the sketch, pixel-based type of input not the CAD vector and element kind of input when actually designing. So for those drawings that we examined in the previous chapter which make the greatest impact on the design process itself, which certainly include proposition, fabulous and experiential drawings, the traditional CAD system is useless. In fact it is relegated in its usefulness to presentation, and instruction drawings and some diagrams. Actually it has many advantages over hand drafting but we will not go into those here.

The problem now is that the sketching interface has given us only pixel information. Quite simply the computer is not holding data that even begins to resemble the knowledge the designer is working with. The fact that some pixels are clustered together to make up a line or an arc is clearly vital knowledge to the designer but this is currently missing the computer. Getting the drawing into the computer in this state gives us no advantage. It can do nothing very useful for us other than store and reproduce.

So the problem is we want the sketch type interface but some kind of component-based knowledge system behind it. Recently we have seen a way of doing this effectively demonstrated by the various methods used for text input on palm pen interfaces. The computer here is given some topological rules about each letter as it is represented in the special character set. Provided as you draw it you do not break those rules, even though you are fairly rough the computer will recognize the letter. In more advanced systems the computer 'learns' your particular style. Mark Gross (1994) has perhaps pushed harder than anyone at the barriers to using the computer for proposition drawings. He has been trying to write programs that can work on these principles but without a restricted character set such as an alphabet so that it might be useful when sketching (Gross, 1996). He is clearly making some progress but we are still in the very primitive stages of making all this as immediate, sensory and flexible as the pencil and paper.

The point here is not the intricacies of the computer systems we will need to make this really buzz but what we can learn from this about what designers know and how they are representing when they draw. Already it is apparent that the designer who is sketching is performing some pretty clever mental operations. An object in the mind is shown as it would appear in the conventions of the drawing which is being worked on. This might be a perspective or it might be a plan or section and so on. This is pretty impressive stuff. Let us just be clear that we recognize it all and give full credit to the huge unseen mental effort behind it. However, now the CAD system in addition wants the designer to work out how each mark is to be constructed from its restricted palette of elements. It is no wonder that extra intrusion is hardly welcome!

The computer as a negative force

But this is not simply an elegant theoretical argument about knowledge representation. Having to work with a computer tool that does not represent knowledge the way you do may cause considerable interference in your thinking. Vinod Goel (1995), to whom we have previously made several references, has compared the way designers work using ordinary manual sketches with the way they work using very simple computer drafting programs of the vectoring type, namely in this case MacDraw. Six graphic designers were set the task of designing tourist posters while six industrial designers were asked to design a desk clock and a toddler's toy. Goel analysed all the drawings produced by both groups of subjects using both manual and computer-based drawing systems. He showed that the drawings done with MacDraw were less dense and less ambiguous than those completed by hand. Perhaps this will not surprise anyone with any skill in drawing who has tried to use such software.

Much more significantly though he also showed that from the design protocols this in turn had an impact on the nature of the design thinking likely to affect the eventual outcome. These differences show that the designers using MacDraw made significantly fewer 'lateral transformations' than their manual sketching counterparts. That is to say they tended to persist with an idea for longer 'vertically transforming' it. The inference here is that the less ambiguous MacDraw system allowed the designers less opportunity to 'see' different interpretations of their drawings. As a result fewer ideas were explored in the process in roughly the same period of time.

Another similar investigation by Bilda and Demirkan (2002) tested designers on an interior design task using both manual and a vectoring-based CAD system known as Design Apprentice. Here a retrospective reporting technique was used to get subjects to recall and describe their intentions by watching a video tape of the protocol. This study again showed fewer 'cognitive actions' as the authors refer to them when using the digital media. The general lesson here seems to align with both experience and behaviour. A general common sense account of experience with such systems is that they are not helpful tools to use while in the early stages of designing. Behaviour suggests that they are not used by designers in this way in spite of having been available for many years. A reasonable conclusion we may draw here is that the existing vectoring CAD systems use symbolic representations that do not map well onto the internal mental symbolic representations used by designers. As a result working with such systems leads to a less rich mental world since the drawings 'talk back' to us in less suggestive ways.

What the drawing represents

But our problems do not stop here. Those experienced in teaching design will be familiar with the problems of working with students who simply draw lines without any real sense of what they represent. The whole point about a drawing done during design is that it is representing something in order to examine and then possibly confirm, maybe reject, or very often refine, or adjust it. Again the refinements and adjustments appear to be made to the drawing but in fact are in reality being made in the designer's mind to the imagined object. Once we ask designers to work with CAD systems they rub up against them in uncomfortable ways and begin to report their difficulties to us enabling us to see more clearly what knowledge they are manipulating. It is clear from this that designers, at least once they are proficient and experienced, are relying heavily on knowledge about the way the objects they are representing behave in terms of their characteristics, the way they are assembled and their affordances. That is to say they are directly interested in the possibilities that arise from using these objects and materials as opposed to the purely abstract geometric representation of them held in the drawing.

Designers are not drawing for the sake of the effect they create, they are not artists in that sense. They are making marks on paper, or here in a computer, which represent something. The wall of a building, the edge of a motor car wheel arch, the outline of a vacuum cleaner and so on. The likelihood is, as we have seen from the previous chapter, that these marks may be vague at some times and precise at other times in the designing process. However, the designer will want to be thinking about what they represent not about some set of complicated rules concerning exactly how you construct a circle or spline curve in the software.

The computer as modeller

A key question we must ask next is about the nature of two- and three-dimensional design knowledge. For those fields of design such as product design, interior or urban design and architecture the designer is not creating graphics at all but three-dimensional form and space. The computer as geometric modeller is really an extension of the drafting role into three dimensions. In these systems therefore there is a further detachment of information from image. Here the user inputs information that first allows the computer to form some kind of three-dimensional model. Later on the computer can then produce a wide variety of drawings of the model in many kinds of projections including plans and perspectives. The latter can of course be rendered as if in particular lighting conditions and so on.

The software depends upon having some mathematical representation of the three-dimensional form from which it can calculate where a particular point is in space. Of course the two-dimensional drafting software has this too. The equation of a straight line or of a circular arc is used to decide how to draw lines and polygons or curves. Freer forms of representation are enabled by spline curves which can have continuously changing radii. In the three-dimensional modeller these are replaced by the more complex equations of planes and curved surfaces. The very first use of such software in architecture tended to be very much tied to planning grids and modularized components. More recently, however, the use of much more sophisticated three-dimensional geometry such as NURBS have enabled the representation of far more free flowing and irregular curves.

It is interesting that the advent of such software has brought some fields of design closer together in their practice. Such curves were always commonplace in naval architecture and in airframe design and indeed in automobile bodies. They have been applied to the smaller items of industrial design such as domestic goods, but now they are also used in architecture. Some very famous names architecturally have recently been building constructions that would have been impossible or highly impractical without computers. Perhaps the highest profile among these is Frank Gehry and his most high profile schemes are the Guggenheim Museum at Bilbao and the Walt Disney Concert Hall in Los Angeles (see Chapter 4). Many of Norman Foster's recent buildings involve geometry which would have been almost impossible to resolve without computers. The significance of this for design might be sensed by looking at Utzon's Sydney Opera House (Fig. 6.1). Utzon did not have such software available to him and his original competition winning drawings showed a set of curved surfaces much less regular than those we come to know in the constructed building. As Weston (2002) points out when the structural engineer Ove Arup was appointed later, he realized that the surfaces would have to be mathematically describable in order to be calculated and constructed. It was only much later that Arup and Utzon found a way of rationalizing these curved surfaces to be segments cut from spheres. Today surfaces much closer to Utzon's original sketch could be mathematically described. However, according to his biographer, Utzon was always looking for a logical surface in relation to his material which was a concrete shell. It seems unlikely that Utzon would have wanted to follow a process similar to that of Gehry.

This sort of CAD is coming as close as we get in architecture to CAD/CAM with its ability to set out individual components for steel structures. Gehry has developed a pattern of building involving steel frames onto which curved cladding is applied. The steel frame members are of course all different in a way that would have been extremely expensive before CAD/CAM. Now, however, they can all be calculated, set out, shaped and even drilled under the

Figure 6.1
Sydney Opera House

digital control of a connected suite of programs. In celebrating this new formal freedom Mitchell (2001) says of Gehry's work:

> His remarkable late projects will ultimately be remembered not only for the spatial qualities and cultural resonances they have achieved, but also for the way in which they have suggested that everyday architectural practice can be liberated from its increasingly sclerotic conventions.

Mitchell is probably right but it is far from just Gehry. For example, the new opera house in Singapore by Michael Wilford is equally free form and equally dependent on computing technology (Fig. 6.2). In essence this is a series of performing spaces and their surrounding circulation spaces which are covered by structures resembling huge glazed upturned kitchen sieves. Such geometry looks simple but is actually extremely complex. Every cell in a kitchen sieve is slightly different from its neighbours as the square grid is resolved onto a curved form. In the tropical climate of Singapore all these cells need shading to avoid the otherwise intolerable solar gain. Every cell also has its own unique orientation and so is partially covered by a uniquely suitable computer designed shade. Such a task would never have been contemplated without computers.

But there are some problems with all this. First, the software that is driven by the complex mathematics of such esoteric devices as Bézier curves or non-uniform rational B-splines is hardly user-friendly. The user of a two-dimensional drafting package can easily enter a line by pointing to either end or a circle by pointing to its centre and any point on its periphery. However, the input of control point locations and tensions on curved patches is not for the

Figure 6.2
Singapore Opera House

faint hearted! It is certainly not intuitive. Such input is very far from the 'conversation with the drawing' discussed in the last chapter. Indeed even Gehry does not work directly on the computer but sculpts physically with much more plastic materials such as paper. In fact Lindsey (2001) tells us that 'Gehry does not like the way objects look in the computer' and that he avoids looking at the computer screens in the office. So all this advance has led to a widespread use of free forms in design but has it really changed the way designers think? Zeara (1995) claims that 'the computer was introduced into Frank Gehry's office in a way that would not interfere with a design process that had been evolving over thirty years'. So such CAD may have altered the designer's thinking inasmuch as more adventurous forms can be contemplated, but whether it has substantially altered the design process itself seems more open to question.

In universities we now commonly see students of architecture presenting schemes that seem designed to show off their prowess on the computer. Such schemes include spectacular examples of rotations, extrusions, and all the manipulative tricks so effortlessly available in the software. This is the architectural equivalent of documents which had every available font in them which we saw a great deal of when the Apple Mac first came out. The skill of a really good designer of course is to edit out such nonsense. It is possible, for example, for an architecture student to gain only a borderline pass for the final thesis design and then win the national CAD prize! Super-realistic computer renderings carry a sort of credibility in our televisual society which hand-drawn images lack. There is a real danger here. Before computers the student architect had to learn to draw in order to design and also in order to see and record. It was of course possible that very poor architecture could be presented so beautifully that one was deceived. But the sensibilities needed to draw well and to design well are sufficiently similar for this hardly ever to happen. Not so now with computers. There may be a danger of deskilling drawing on the computer leaving young designers unable to draw by hand well enough to record and sketch which the last chapter suggested are central activities in the design process. A young student learning to design may well be advised not to rely heavily on CAD in the formative years if that led to neglecting the development of drawing skills so central to design thinking.

The computer as critic

It has long been an ambition in architecture at least, that computers would enable us to improve the predictability of design. Although design by drawing has given the architect more power to experiment than was available to the vernacular craftsman it has not necessarily brought any greater reliability. Drawings are not very good at revealing some of the inadequacies of designs that become all too apparent when they are made and used. So the extension of such an argument must surely be that with computers we can model more features of the design and test it more thoroughly.

So early CAD software for architecture was created to allow the computer effectively to act as design critic. Simple programs could estimate the energy consumption of buildings, for example. Others could calculate the daylight levels or solar gain in rooms anywhere in the world at any time of the year. We could calculate room acoustics and noise transmission. We could estimate the amount of materials required and even the overall capital cost. This would enable us to think about buildings as integrated wholes rather than just as sculptural objects as the CAD modeller does. In fact this vision of the computer as design critic has hardly materialized in terms of the potential because several quite intractable problems have emerged.

John Landsdown (1969) first pointed out that we could have software that was 'ad-hoc' or 'integrated'. The advantage with separate and 'ad-hoc' programs would be that each requires its own input and the designer would only have to describe to it those features of the building necessary for it to do its limited job. On the other hand an integrated suite of packages could be served by one single comprehensive building model. From the design process point of view the latter seems more desirable as it enables holistic thinking and it has remained the ambition of many software developers to realize it.

The first problem is that the time taken to input all this information is such that you can really only afford to do it once the design is pretty well finalized. This too is one of the main obstacles to using virtual reality in design. This then is not computer-aided design but computer-checked design or computer-visualized design. The computer is certainly acting as a design critic but rather too late in the process to be constructive.

Conceptual structures

The second problem is that when you are designing you need to interact with the representation you are using in a variety of mental modalities (Lawson and Roberts, 1991). Architects it seems unselfconsciously think about their building in several ways while they are designing. Listen to any conversation between architects about buildings that they are either designing or examining and you will hear evidence of this in almost every sentence. They talk about conceptual structures such as spaces, circulation systems or external skins. It is actually very hard to pin down just which physical components belong to these structures and which do not. More problematically the conceptual structures are so organized that any one physical component may belong to many of them (Fig. 6.3).

Let us examine this in a little more detail. A building can be seen as a collection of spaces which may be indoors, outdoors or hybrids such as courtyards and atria. Alternatively a building can be seen as a collection of systems such as those for human circulation, those that provide structural stability. There are those that form the external skin or the building core, they may be the collected services for environmental control or for safety and so on. Let us note in passing how complicated this is already since in a framed building a wall may form part of the external skin but not the structure whereas in load-bearing construction it most certainly would. Note also that some internal walls or doors may form part of the fire safety system and others not. You need a great deal of knowledge in order to work all this out, but nevertheless it may be

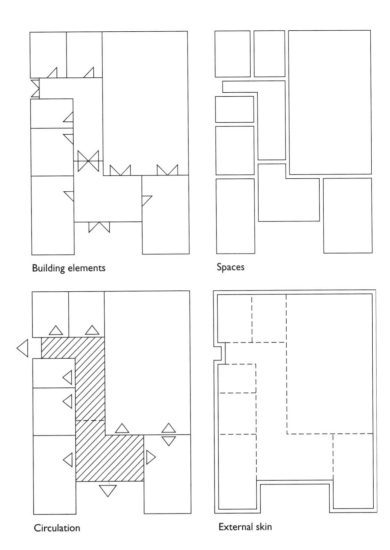

Building elements

Spaces

Circulation

External skin

Figure 6.3
Four different ways of knowing about the same simple building

quite readily apparent to an architect simply looking at some drawings or walking around the building. An example of the same architect representing a design in different modes during the design process can be seen in Figs 6.4 and 6.5. Here Robert Venturi is working on plan proposition drawings for his design for the extension to the National Gallery in London. One plan clearly shows Venturi thinking in spatial mode (Fig. 6.4) and the other in building element or component mode (Fig. 6.5). (Other drawings for this project appear in Chapter 4.)

We have started to mention components which offer an obvious way of representing the building. It can be seen as a collection of building elements such as walls, windows, doors and roofs. It turns out that these elements are in themselves problematic to encode. Some, like windows, may be genuine components fully defined geometrically by their specification. However, others, like walls, may be generic surfaces sharing a common section and yet with each actual physical instance being geometrically unique. Other building elements

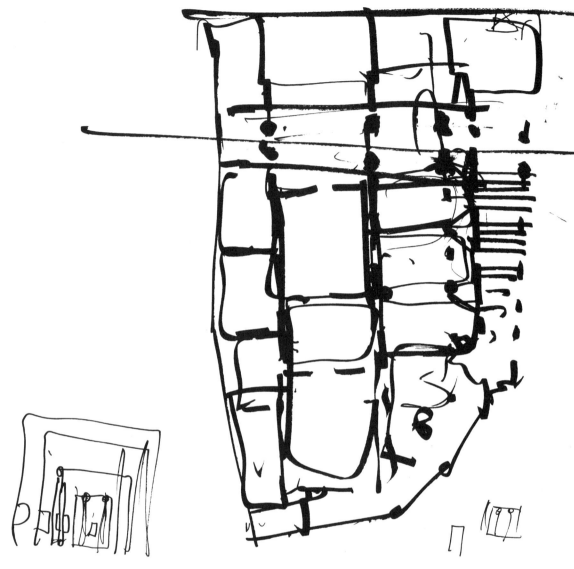

Figure 6.4
An example of a spatial mode drawing by Robert Venturi of his design for the National Gallery Extension in London

may be junction details such as eaves or verges with each instance varying only from the others by its length.

There are probably many more ways of thinking about buildings. Some of them even relate to the way they are commonly represented. For example, we also commonly think of buildings to be comprised of layers such as floor levels or sections.

When designing we oscillate without noticing between these descriptions of the building. This is easy and unselfconscious when sketching. However, computer systems invariably demand that we talk to them using their own

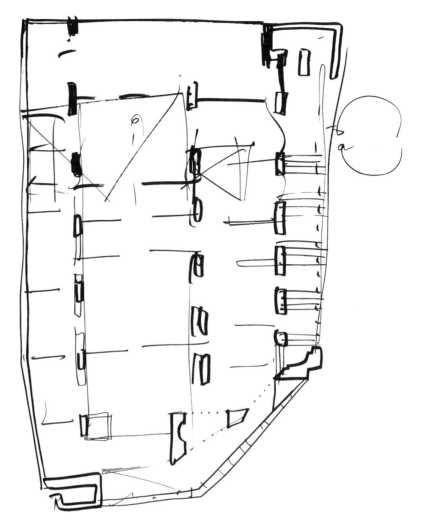

Figure 6.5
Another example for the same
project as Fig. 6.4 but this time
showing a component mode view

library of components. Often these are just that, components which must first be described and then positioned. While designing, one seldom thinks that way at least to begin with. So while interacting with a computer system the designer often has to interrupt actual productive and creative thought by translating all this into the restricted unimodal computer language. The research of my team has shown that a multimodal computer building model is possible and we have written translators between the spatial, component, system and layer modes (Lawson and Riley, 1982). These ideas were partially implemented in an early CAD system called GABLE. However, getting a computer to fully, automatically and accurately understand all the modes of thought about a building that an architect uses is probably not a realizable goal. This comes remarkably close to the task of total natural language translation which as we shall see later requires knowledge beyond the given material. We shall return to this problem in the final chapter.

Modellers and carvers

All this tells us that designers know something about the real world materials and objects they are working with. More importantly, good designers seem to work with the nature of those materials and objects rather than against it. The art critic Adrian Stokes (1934) used a lovely distinction between what he called 'modelling' and 'carving'. In this context he probably would have said that our existing CAD systems are 'modellers' and it is interesting that we call them that. Perhaps what creative designers really need are CAD 'carvers'. A carver works with the grain, sometimes literally, but always at least metaphorically. It is a reflective process in which the nature of the material being worked on is an important influence on the final form. CAD modelling systems have none of that quality since they treat all objects as free of the constraints of any materiality. In reality wall and roof surfaces, courtyards or rooms all have characteristics and beautiful ones are 'carved' out showing an appreciation of their natural language. Some designers are more sensitive to this than others perhaps with Eva Jiricna, Santiago Calatrava and Carlo Scarpa among those discussed here very obvious examples of 'carvers' who generate form very much from an understanding of the materials they work with. Calatrava certainly uses computers for finite element analysis and other structural calculations (Lawson, 1994). He admires 'the unbelievable precision with which you can construct lines or arcs'. He also appreciates the value of computer modelling systems allied to sophisticated rendering but does not himself like to use even these. 'I do not want to have an abstraction, I don't want to have a hyper-realistic model but one that is really blank.' He greatly prefers to make physical models rather than using computer modelling systems because they are 'so much more direct'. Clearly the fact that Calatrava uses computers for other purposes suggests that this is no Luddite anti-technology tendency. It is simply that the software we have so far is not able to allow him think creatively while using it.

However, there are some encouraging signs that some of these problems may be at least partly solvable. Jim Glymph is Frank Gehry's partner and the principal of Gehry Technologies, which develops the computing side of their work. His group are working on computer modelling that does indeed have some knowledge about materiality. Although Gehry's designs may look entirely free, to realize them does depend not on construction in paper but in concrete and metal. In particular there are constraints about the curvature of panels and the rates of change of curvature. Glymph talks of building such knowledge into computer programs that enable the designer to work with the elasticity and other characteristics of the real materials (Glymph, 2004). Such programs could indeed facilitate a 'carver' rather than purely 'modeller' approach to design thinking.

Deskilling design

Earlier we saw a possible danger of the deskilling of drawing as a result of using computers, but we should perhaps recognize the other side of this coin.

Today many programs are available to help ordinary people who are not professional designers to express and organize their design ideas. In addition to the generic drafting and modelling programs already discussed there are kitchen planners, garden planners and so on all available off the shelf or even over the Internet. An early experiment by Robert Aish remains a fascinating demonstration of the possible power of such an application of technology to design. Aish used the simple suite of programs developed at Strathclyde University to sketch and evaluate building designs. They were quite restricted geometrically but required little skill to operate. They could not only reproduce a drawing neatly but also gave some indication of the performance of the emerging building against a limited number of criteria such as circulation efficiency, floor area, crude costs and so on.

Aish used these programs to get experimental subjects to design a nursery school. What makes these experiments so fascinating was the inclusion of nursery school head teachers among the subjects. These head teachers had no experience either of architectural design or of computing, but could perform this task using the programs provided (Aish, 1977):

> The participant can produce a graphically accurate drawing of his design idea while the calculative aspects of the program perform a value free tutorial role and help him to bring his design within cost and performance limits

Encouragingly, the results of the study showed that when the teachers were involved in using the program, the designs were judged (by other teachers) as more satisfactory interpretations of user needs. Of course, this is not to say these were 'better' designs in any general sense. What it does suggest is that somehow the teachers using the software were able to enshrine knowledge about what makes a good school in their designs that they were unable to communicate sufficiently clearly to enable the professional designer to do so.

Co-ordinating and managing design information

There is no doubt that computers offer huge potential in terms of information management. Design is after all a process of creating, manipulating and managing information. Much can go wrong unless we get this right. As time goes on this has become even more critical with design teams not co-located, with increasing specialization, with faster speed of production required and ever greater efficiency aimed for. And yet as long ago as a quarter of a century research showed that the failure to co-ordinate drawings in architecture was one of the major causes of all on-site contractual problems leading to delay or additional cost or both (Crawshaw, 1976). As large complex objects such as buildings are designed over long periods of time, changes take place as the drawings are being produced. We often have very poor ways of ensuring that a change is properly reflected in all the documents in which it appears. It is surprisingly easy for a staircase to appear in quite different places on different floor level plans, for example! Computer drafting has undoubtedly enabled much higher levels of control over drawn information especially when produced by many people in many places. However, the comprehensive computer system that models the object in all three dimensions and then generates the various views such as plans, sections and elevations automatically remains the goal. Such systems exist but have not yet been able to sustain early design creative thinking as we saw earlier in the chapter.

One of the most glaring deficiencies in the conventional design process is the lack of relationship between the original brief of the client and the final drawings produced by the designer. It may be the case that the design satisfies the brief or not, but it is extraordinarily difficult for a client to check this especially in the case of large complex projects such as buildings. The knowledge about why a design solution is the way it is and how this relates to the brief is not built into the solution itself. Indeed it may be lost to the design team too. The architect Michael Wilford told me that at one of the meetings near the completion of his Temasek Polytechnic in Singapore he looked around the room and was astonished to realize that he was the only person present who had sat in on the very first meeting! Large complex designed objects of this kind worked on by teams create huge knowledge management problems.

Recently some research has begun to use computers to capture the rationale behind decisions as they are taken during the process (Cerulli *et al.*, 2001). This not only allows the client to make checks on progress at the end, but also enables the members of a multi-professional design team to understand what all the other specialists are doing and why. In the modern conventional design process, for example, it is perfectly possible for an architect to draw a plan which goes to both structural and services engineers. Simultaneously the structural engineer may be thickening a column on this plan just as the services engineer is planning to run a duct past it. Detecting such clashes is possible with a comprehensive 3D CAD system. However, deciding what to do about it may be facilitated by a design rationale capturing system.

Networks

All this suggests that not just computers but also their networks deserve our attention. It is the ability to transfer information from one place to another in a variety of ways that makes the network so powerful as an information management tool. As Bill Mitchell points out at the head of this chapter the Net has quite different rules to conventional physical places. Already we are seeing design proceed around the world as one team passes information to another so that a project is kept permanently active in successive time zones.

As a result, a large amount of current research is concerned with how computers may be able to facilitate the necessary co-operation between members of design teams (Peng, 1994). Traditional forms of communication are either one to one or one to many. Local and wide area networks offer the possibility of many to many communication, and the chance to communicate with people who are unknown to you. Many of these forms of communication, such as electronic mail, are also asynchronous compared with the traditional telephone call which requires caller and receiver to communicate at the same time. Electronic mail is more like a letter which arrives almost instantly it is sent but can be read at any time. These characteristics are likely to make networks helpful in the sort of group collaborative situations found in the design process. We shall return to some of these issues in subsequent chapters on designing with others and on design conversations.

We are likely to see the development of computer tools which we might call agents. Such tools will be able to act for us in much the same way as a travel agent or an insurance agent does. They will know where to look for information and come back to us only with that which we need to know. A good travel agent may not just organize a trip when you require it, but may also be on the lookout for special deals or opportunities which might appeal to you. So it will be with our software agents. They will learn what kinds of information interest us and how important they might be. They will probably learn to deal with the software agents of other people on the networks and thus propagate messages about our interests.

Given that design is such a knowledge-rich activity, these developments could have quite profound and fundamental effects on the design professions. Clients and their design professionals will be able to find each other and communicate in quite new ways. Design is almost invariably a team activity requiring a great deal of information to flow between collaborators. We are only just beginning to explore the possible ways in which networks of computers can support collaborative work. The roles designers play could very easily be redefined in such a world. It is quite possible that the effect of networks will ultimately have much more of an impact on the design process than has the single humble computer. For now what we can see from all this is that developing computer systems that share knowledge with designers in ways that they find normal, helpful and understandable is extremely difficult. Creating such systems may be more problematic than we thought when CAD first raised the possibly of aiding design and creative thought. Making progress with this great project is also likely to teach us much more about the kinds of knowledge that designers work with and how.

7

Design conversations

Language can become a screen that stands between the thinker and reality.
That is the reason why true creativity starts where language ends.

Arthur Koestler

a reflective conversation with the situation

Donald Schön

Design is generally a pretty collaborative business. Another of the reasons why the protocol analysis work is problematic is because it tends on the whole to explore design as something that goes on inside a single designer's head. Admittedly some design protocols at least involve groups of designers, but they seldom involve clients, users, legislators, consultants, suppliers and manufacturers. In fact design in the real world happens with all these people involved and we neglect that dimension at our peril.

When two or more people are involved in a design process they must talk to each other about it. In this chapter we shall examine such conversations and also explore the powerful idea that design thinking may itself be conversational in nature. Donald Schön has developed a powerful view of design as reflective practice. In such a view the reflection can be seen as a conversation with the situation, often conducted through the drawing. Kees Dorst (1997) has produced a thorough and interesting comparison of this paradigm with the more conventional problem-solving view.

My research group has become progressively more interested in design conversations as we have come to realize they offer powerful insights into the mental activity that normally remains hidden from us when designers think in a solitary and introspective fashion. One of my group decided to try to design a program that would enable a computer to hold a meaningful design conversation (Lawson and Loke, 1997). The test of success we decided would be whether a designer could talk to it about design and find the conversation interesting and useful. Of course we were not really trying to create such a program but rather trying to understand what elements and characteristics it would need in order to pass our test (Fig. 7.1).

Loke Shee Ming, who was doing this work, progressed it to the point where he had identified many constituent elements of the program and could describe their characteristics. So he gave a seminar on the work in progress for discussion in the group. A colleague who was primarily interested in computer-aided design was at the seminar and became rather impatient and dismissive about

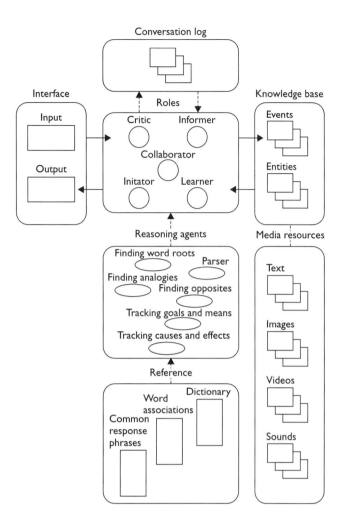

Figure 7.1
A design conversation system

the work. We were concentrating on the wrong things he said. 'Go into any design studio and 99% of what you would see will be drawings', he claimed. My response was to point out that probably 100 per cent of what you would hear would be words! So far in the literature on the design process, our conversations about design have been rather neglected. This is probably because they disappear into 'thin air' as it were. There is often little or no evidence of them having taken place and they are seldom recorded except in the rather formal language of written correspondence. Such language of course becomes even more tortuous and long-winded when set in the framework of a legal contract and when the participants are conscious of the need to protect themselves from possible litigation.

Some researchers interested in language have started to explore design conversations and arrived at some rather interesting preliminary conclusions. Medway and Andrews (1992) have studied a real recorded conversation in an architects' office between three partners of the practice. The context in which this conversation takes place is that one of the partners has just returned from holiday and is being briefed about the progress of the project in his absence. During the conversation other offshoots occur as one of the partners takes phone calls to discuss the same matters. The linguistic analysis presented of this conversation raises several points of relevance to us here. First, Medway and Andrews note that the 'base mode of the conversation is narrative'. That is to say that although from time to time the conversational mode changes temporarily, it begins in and generally returns to a style similar to that of telling a story. We shall return to the idea of design as narrative shortly. Second, this analysis shows that there is frequent reference to documents throughout the conversation. This is hardly astonishing in itself but what is of particular interest to these linguistic researchers is the way in which the designers when treating drawn and written documents 'regard them as equivalent'. This clearly surprises those steeped in linguistic research. 'That architecture is such a textual business is not what we expected to emerge from our close analysis of the transcripts.' However, let us be careful here. In terms of the analysis we conducted of drawings in Chapter 4 the drawings referred to here were 'presentation drawings'. Drawings had been done for clients and to obtain planning consent. These were not 'proposition drawings' done as part of the decision-making process of the designers themselves. In this sense it is quite reasonable that designers refer to such drawings just as they would written texts. It would be interesting to see this kind of research applied to the generation and content of design drawings and sketches.

A picture is worth a thousand words ... but not always!

In fact the use of words rather than graphical images can offer distinct advantages during the design process. There are times when the drawing seems either redundant or even harmful to the communication process. When British Rail wanted to develop a new design for their InterCity trains they invited a number of leading designers to submit proposals. The winners were in fact Seymour/Powell who at that time had no previous experience with train design. The Seymour/Powell submission was not based on drawings or traditional design documents. They simply explained to British Rail that their design would be 'heroic' in the manner of the British Airways Concorde and that it would once again make children want to become train drivers as in early times. We can only imagine that such a description must have triggered childhood memories in the minds of some senior British Rail executives, and that they carried with them their own image of such a train. Had Seymour/Powell shown drawings or a model they may have unwittingly indicated some features that clashed with the mental images in the minds of their clients. Once commissioned, Seymour/Powell were able to take a much more detailed brief and set about designing the InterCity 250 which in due course may well be re-created in model form and sold to countless would-be train drivers!

The architect Eva Jiricna is known for her stunning interiors often based on high technology materials. She has described how her design process depends very much on a phase of communication with her clients which relies on verbal rather than graphical media. She tells how 'I try to express in words what they [the clients] want, and then I try to twist it into a different statement and then draw it' (Lawson, 1994). Through this device Eva has managed to produce entirely modern designs with which her clients are quite happy even though they may have originally expressed their wish for historical restoration. Such results are obviously due not only to Eva's extraordinary talent but also the great care she takes to explain and to educate her clients. However, it seems unlikely that she could achieve these ends by using drawings in her early communications. The verbal description allows her clients to interpret shades of meaning not allowed by the drawing. In the same way we can easily be disappointed by the film of a book we have previously read. During the reading we will have built up our own image of the characters and places which the film has no alternative but to contradict. Careful and sensitive management of the client through this difficult period of imagining the design seems to be one of the hallmarks of successful designers.

Designers and design students report quite commonly that they often feel the need *not* to draw. It seems that when an idea occurs to us we may feel that the drawing will force us to clarify it too quickly. It sometimes seems better to let an idea mature a little before testing it too hard with the drawing.

In this context it may be worth recalling the lessons of Chapter 4 in which we saw how 'design by drawing' is a relatively recent phenomenon. The vernacular process characteristically involved little or no drawing. In his entertaining account of the life, times and work of a Purbeck stone worker, Eric Benfield (1940) presents almost no drawings at all. Indeed at one point he comments that:

> Most plans were and are carried in the head, and there are some unlikely looking heads around in Swanage which could tell a good deal about the fields that are now ignorantly being built over.

This may, in our age of the graphical image, seem a rather perverse attitude, after all a picture is supposed to be worth a thousand words. However, there are some ways in which a picture can often carry too much information or indicate a degree of precision which may be inappropriate. This is illustrated again by Benfield's description of how to build a stone bird bath or sundial:

> A bird bath or sundial should be about two and a half times as high as it is wide in the base; preferably it should have two or three bases, which give the effect of steps usually seen around village crosses, and a shorter tapering pedestal surmounted by a bath smaller than the bases by at least two inches.

In this text-based description Benfield only tells a stone mason that which it is necessary to know and leaves entirely free to the imagination all other detail. This is a remarkably clever and precisely judged transmission of design knowledge. It would be difficult to construct a drawing that did not suggest other features of the form of the finished product which might restrict a future designer. A similar lack of enthusiasm for overprescriptive drawings can be found running through the pages of George Sturt's description of the designs of cartwheels which was referred to in Chapter 2. These two vernacular designers are following in the footsteps of the great Leon Battista Alberti who in 1550 published his ten books on architecture, *De re aedificatoria*, which in their original version were entirely without illustration. Perhaps all these early authors suffered from a lack of reprographic technology, but the effectiveness and, in Alberti's case, longevity of their work are testimony to the power of words to convey design ideas.

Drawing and talking

We have already made reference to the remarkable series of studies organized by Nigel Cross in which a substantial number of research workers were asked to analyse the same set of design protocols (Cross *et al.*, 1996). These protocols were video recordings of designers working either independently or in groups. The beauty of such data is that, particularly in the case of the design groups, the words are recorded alongside the drawings and we can study what was said as drawings were being made.

In his own study, Nigel Cross (1996) points out the importance of the conjunction between drawing and talking in design groups. In his study the design group were trying to design a device for carrying a hiker's backpack on a mountain bicycle. Cross points out that well over an hour into the design process one member of the group introduced a design concept with the words 'maybe it's like a little vacuum-formed tray'. Prior to this point the team had been using the word 'bag' as a way of describing to each other what they were trying to create. As with Benfield's description of the sundial, the word tray was sufficiently evocative without being too prescriptive, and this word then continues to be used by all the members of the team in turn as they draw alternative interpretations of how this might work.

In fact Cross's paper is full of examples of how drawing and talking together make the design process work. Cross also points out that by studying both together we can see the development of design ideas not necessarily as creative 'leaps' but as 'bridges' between ideas as the words enable transitions between ideas which look abruptly different if we only look at the drawings. Both words and pictures have their advantages, but combined they offer a very powerful 'language of design'.

Conversational roles

Most conversations are forms of collaboration. For example, it simply does not work if we all talk at the same time. Generally we take it in turns when talking to just one other person. When there is a larger group this can get difficult unless the participants all maintain a sense of fairness and a spirit of collaboration, giving each other opportunities to speak, not interrupting too frequently and so on. Eventually in more formal decision-making situations we may need to introduce a chairing role to police this and ensure the conversation stays focused, productive, and co-operative. However, in less formal settings such as the design studio the participants must understand and respect the roles the others are playing at the time. We found when studying design conversations that there are at least five quite distinct and fundamentally important roles frequently adopted. We call these roles 'learner', 'informer', 'critic', 'collaborator' and 'initiator'. In fact these roles serve to structure and organize creative conversations which would otherwise become chaotic and confusing. Participants usually play their roles according to cues (such as words or gestures) given by others. In some cases, participants may choose to ignore the cues in order to bring a certain emphasis to what they are saying. The choice of a role is a matter of how one sees oneself in a situation, or in other words, the consciousness of 'self'.

Let us now examine the characteristics of these design conversation roles. The 'learner' is one who absorbs what others say and remembers or learns. The 'informer' answers others' queries. The 'critic' checks the validity of what others have said and makes comment on it, giving warning occasionally. The 'collaborator' tries to elaborate and build on what others have said rather than criticizing. Finally, the 'initiator' begins a new conversational thread or develops a new perspective on the subject when the others have no more to say.

Let us see how these roles might work during a conversation about a design. Le Corbusier might have begun such a conversation by telling us that 'a house is a machine for living in'. A 'learner' would record this association and request explanation of any words not understood. A 'critic' might have reminded him of the differences between a house and a machine, perhaps replying 'a house has rooms and furniture but a machine does not'. A 'collaborator' role might have tried to extend or elaborate the metaphor of the house as machine by suggesting that 'a house performs functions' or perhaps 'a house uses fuel'. Finally, an 'initiator' might have given a new direction to the discussion by suggesting that 'a family lives in a house' thus focusing attention on the occupants rather than the building.

In a chapter on Designing with Others in *How Designers Think* I described how in design groups people tend habitually to adopt character roles (Lawson, 1997). Such roles include those of 'leader', 'clown', 'critic', 'lawyer', 'dunce' and so on. It is now possible to relate these two sets of ideas and see that 'leaders' in design groups are likely to appear to initiate, 'clowns' may appear to be a 'critic' and might be able to do this in a way that does not cause offence because of the humour attached to the role. The 'lawyer' by comparison may appear to criticize more negatively but may also collaborate by developing ideas within limits permitted by legislation or costs and so on. The 'dunce' may often play the learner role by appearing to be in need of further explanation. Such a device can often force an idea to be clarified and simultaneously give the initiating 'leader' more credibility.

Thus conversations that are well structured by a group of people playing out their roles and yet sharing the same goals can become a powerful creative force. It is, however, also possible to see how easily all this can fall apart if the roles are misused. Learning to develop the conversational modes is clearly one of the most important things a creative group must do. However, clearly it is necessary to understand something of these roles and how they are being played in the context of a particular group if one is to make sense of the way knowledge is being acquired, developed, explored and communicated.

Conversations of the mind

Earlier in this book and in more detail elsewhere (Lawson, 1997) I have argued that maps of the design process are not particularly helpful, as the apparent steps of analysis, synthesis and evaluation they inevitably rely on are likely to take place so cyclically, iteratively and interactively that such maps give a misleading impression of direction. In fact it is probably more realistic to see the design process as a kind of negotiation between problem and solution, and that problems are not necessarily understood by designers in advance of them generating solutions. So just how does this negotiation take place?

Obviously design solutions and problems are themselves entirely inanimate and cannot actually take part in a process of negotiation. We have been discussing design as a form of collaboration which it often is in creative teams. However, even when design takes place inside a single mind we can still imagine it to be in the form of a conversation.

Donald Schön (1983) has suggested very helpfully that designers 'have a conversation with the situation'. In simple terms he suggests that designers draw and react to their drawings. In essence the drawings speak back to them and appear to suggest further steps that could be taken. This interesting idea effectively characterises design thinking as the holding of an internal conversation. In fact Schön did not originally develop this notion specifically in order to describe design but to depict a wider range of activities which he characterized as 'reflective practice'.

The idea of talking to ourselves is hardly a strange one. Which of us does not occasionally catch ourselves muttering or even talking out loud in such situations? This is recognizable to most of us as something we do not just in design but in many situations where we are trying to think something through. Of course we may be more aware of doing this at some times than others. Ultimately we may 'think aloud' and actually verbalize the internal conversation. Occasionally perhaps we are 'caught out' 'talking to ourselves' by a neighbour who may comment on it and only then do we realize how concrete this conversation with ourselves has become.

Narrative design conversations

Conversations cannot meaningfully take place unless there are some shared ideas involving some reasonably well-defined and understood features. If I begin a conversation by saying to you 'this is a nice sunny day', then I do so in the expectation that you understand what a day is and what the sun is. I also expect you to share the concept of niceness with me, and to agree that sunny days are preferable to cloudy ones. Of course I have chosen this example deliberately to involve only everyday almost globally understood matters. In design this is very likely not to be true all of the time. Problematically sometimes, some of those potentially involved in a design conversation may not fully understand all of the matters under consideration. Alternatively they may understand them in such a different way from others in the conversation that it cannot be productive.

Conversations can take on a number of quite different characteristics and real everyday conversations often go through a number of such phases. What distinguishes these phases from each other is the relative roles that the participants play. It seems likely that design conversations are no different in this respect and indeed research confirms this. Perhaps the most basic and obvious conversation phase is the telling of a story or 'narrative'. Here at least one participant is in what we might think of as the 'informer' role. He or she is imparting information to the others. In the context of a design team Medway and Andrews (1992) showed that reasons for this include bringing them up to date or seeking a reaction or needing to agree something. In narrative a number of features may be present. We may introduce characters, places or objects. We may describe events. We may set up situations in which events are played out by characters in places with objects.

So it is in design conversations. Part of them involves the need to identify components, elements or features. Schön in his work calls this 'naming'. Recently design research has taken more interest in design conversations as revealed by the recorded protocols of designers either in the real world or in the laboratory (Cross et al., 1996). One such set of protocols was collected by Faisal Agabani (1980) who asked pairs of architecture students to work together and video taped the process. The students were asked to design a children's nursery, they were given a written brief and shown a video of the site. The first comment made by one of these students was 'the most important thing is that we are going to have children playing outside'. Now this comment is stating, many of us might feel overstating, a part of the problem as this designer saw it. Whether or not overall this is indeed 'the most important thing' is highly questionable. However, that is not the point that is of most interest to us here. We are used to designers making such statements which 'frame' the problem in a particular way. At this stage we can see this as a process of 'identification'. If we see the conversation as a narrative then we are in one of the very early sections of the story where characters are named, identified and introduced. The same designer continued: 'so which way round do you put all the playing areas so they can wander around safely?' Here the designer is now exploring the problem and framing it in terms of the previous statement. This sentence starts to explore the character of the play areas. What does it mean to have an outdoor play area and how might it impact on other parts of the problem? These are questions being asked. Importantly the narrative has now seamlessly moved into a solution-oriented discourse. We have already arrived at what we might call a design focus or situation. Schön uses the term 'framing' to describe this process although he is far from clear as to exactly what constitutes a 'frame'.

There seem to be several reasons why such a 'framing' process is an important and central feature of design thinking. First, although design is integrative, it is often not possible to think about the totality of the problem or indeed the solution at all times. It simply is too complex and confusing a matter. Instead designers seem to narrow their attention by setting up a situation, focusing, or 'framing'.

These structuring ideas are commonly found in design protocols, whether we call them 'frames', 'primary generators', or in the more common parlance of the design studio 'partis'. Indeed they seem to be the very essence of design thinking and at the heart of the design process. They do not necessarily appear logically out of some objective analysis of the design problem. Indeed they may be unique to that particular design problem as perceived by that particular designer or designers at that particular time and stage of the process. Experience shows quite clearly that other designers may have used quite different ideas, and even the same designers may feel quite differently at different stages in the same process as they learn more about the situation. So it is of course with all conversations. At one stage in a conversation one set of ideas may dominate and structure the whole topic, but it is likely that the focus will change as the conversation develops and quite different, perhaps even conflicting, ways of structuring the issue will take their turn on the stage as it were.

Let us return to Agabani's architecture students designing their nursery school. The next thing to be said by the other student collaborating here was: 'well we could make the building "L" shaped and use the angle to protect the play areas'. In Schön's terminology our designers have now passed on to the next phase of design thinking which he calls 'moving'. Quite simply they have proposed a solution characteristic but it is based solely on the current 'frame'. Later quite normally this design idea is rejected for other reasons as other frames come into operation. In fact in this particular protocol the shape is drawn and the other student comments that: 'yes but the way round the site is the play area would be in shade not in the sun'. Remember that these students were designing for Sheffield in the United Kingdom where summer sun is seen as desirable! However, again importantly what has happened here is that a new characteristic of the play area has been introduced. Not only must it be protected and secure but it should also be sunny. As the students progress they rapidly move on to concerns that have nothing to do with the outdoor play space at all: 'doing it that way round how would we make a good entrance?' Here a new character, the entrance, has been identified. Soon of course they are concerned with the features of entrances and the problem is rapidly reframed and more moves are made. The conversation develops and the story gradually emerges as all the characters make their appearance.

Listen to any conversation and you find a great deal of just this sort of story telling. But also you will hear sudden leaps and changes as one idea triggers another apparently remote from it. Anecdotes, recollections of previous events, momentous occasions, amusing incidents, unusual occurrences, any of these and many more will come into the minds of the conversationalists as they talk. So it seems there is yet another important parallel with the design process and conversations.

From the various recorded examples of design conversation and from a series of interviews with designers (Lawson, 1994) it has become apparent that designers use words in special ways when they know they are talking to other designers. Here they are communicating design concepts which they either know or assume will be shared territory as it were. The words are selected carefully to evoke and communicate subtleties of design concepts which would take many words and drawings to explain to an outsider but which might be summarized in short phrases or even single words. The evocativeness of words is the key. Schön (1988) suggested that experienced designers use design archetypes during their design process often in the form of very evocative words.

A design lexicon

This may leave designers with a problem when conversing with their clients or users who may not share this lexicon. In fact it has been suggested that the commonly felt lack of character in the twentieth century-built landscape is due to the insufficient vocabularies of graphically oriented designers to describe and evoke multifaceted design possibilities and emotional responses, so others who are involved in implementing their ideas cannot share their visions (Hodges, 1991).

In this chapter we have seen several examples of highly evocative words being used in design conversations. Seymour/Powell's 'heroic' train, Benfield's 'village cross', and Nigel Cross's 'bag' and 'tray' all clearly triggered complex sets of ideas in the minds of those who heard them. How do words become evocative? Of course this is really a question about memory and how we store and recall information from it. It has long been recognized that we have several memory systems and the distinction between long- and short-term memory is a familiar one. The evocativeness of words is a function of our long-term memory which is conceptual and schemata based (Bartlett, 1932). A schema can be a complex idea or concept which can be seen as a series of slots into which values can be inserted to represent particular cases. So the schema for a 'dog' will define it as having four legs, a tail that wags, capable of making a barking sound and so on. However, not all dogs are the same, so each of these and all the other slots in our complex schema can have particular values from which we recognize an animal not only as a dog but, as we get more expert, as a particular breed, and even as a unique creature. As we develop these schemata become more elaborate and distinct. A young child may not be able to distinguish between dogs, horses and cows. A dog breeder will recognize many more breeds than an average person. So designers just like dog breeders develop more sophisticated and elaborated schemata for the concepts they work with frequently.

However, this memory system has many cognitive advantages not least of which is its ability to recall the schema from individual slots of information. Motor car enthusiasts on a recent television programme in the UK were shown to be able to recognize makes of motor car from tiny fragments of the body-work form. Similarly an architect may recognize a building by a particular designer perhaps even without recognizing the building itself and possibly without having seen it before.

This characteristic of memory allows words to become metonymic. Here a word representing a characteristic of something eventually comes to stand for the whole thing. We talk of the 'top brass' as the highest ranking officers in the military because their uniform has more metal than the lower ranks. The word 'birthday' thus evokes for you not only its technical meaning of the anniversary of your birth but also parties, presents, friends and relatives and actual events that have occurred on your birthday (Rumelhart and Norman, 1983). Each schema therefore can be seen as a series of slots, which can hold values to represent specific cases or instances of the schema (Minsky, 1975). When we receive new information through our senses, our memory will try to match it with these mental templates, enabling us to recall the whole schema from any appropriate value of any slot. This helps explain the apparently metonymic nature of such memory. The mere mentioning of 'birthday' brings forth memories of birthday parties, friends and diverse emotions (Schank, 1982).

There is a further argument which suggests that human understanding of concepts may be built up from very basic bodily experiences accumulated over time through physical interactions with the external world (Lakoff and Johnson, 1980). That is to say we most vividly remember sensations and feelings, including movement. Those who have developed a high level of skill in playing a musical instrument or sport will recognize the importance of this 'body memory'. In discussing the idea that thinking and therefore designing might be a skill that could and should be practised I have often used quotations from books on other skills. I try very hard to play the flute and do so very badly. One of the books I found most helpful tells me what it feels like when you are doing it properly. In other words it supplies a benchmark against which you can test your bodily memory. In fact I play several woodwind instruments and sometimes people ask me if I do not get confused between the different fingering patterns that are needed to make the same notes. The answer is simply no. This is not because I am particularly clever or good at this, but simply the body memory which is triggered by the size, weight and position of the instrument automatically tells me how to finger it.

This theory of memory suggests that there may be problems remembering deeper and more abstract concepts, which cannot be understood simply as bodily experiences. Such concepts, this theory argues, may be understood through the use of one or more metaphors on those directly experienced concepts. Even here then, the argument goes, bodily memory is important.

Metaphor is therefore not merely a literary device but a crucial cognitive mechanism. A good example would be the architect Richard MacCormac's work on the design of his chapel at Fitzwilliam College in Cambridge to which we have already made reference. Central to the whole design process was the metaphor of a 'ship' or 'vessel', leading right down into the detailing of the junctions between materials (Lawson, 1994). While doing research on this designer I visited the office and in the space of one day heard several different people use the word 'belvedere' in conversations with me. Of course this is a perfectly acceptable word, but it is rare in usage and one does not expect to hear it frequently even in architectural circles. What was clear here was that it had come to evoke a very sophisticated set of concepts shared by a whole design team. The team had recently visited some buildings and looked at some designs together and become fascinated by this concept. It was clear that they were not using the word to refer only to conventional examples of buildings constructed purposely to be belvederes, but to any high tower-like construction from which a good view could be obtained. All this is leading us on to a further distinction in memory between that which is symbolic and that which is episodic. Put simply we seem to store information quite differently about theories and rules to the way we remember events and occasions. It turns out that this has enormous significance for understanding the nature of design knowledge. That is the subject of the next chapter.

8

Theoretical and experiential knowledge in design

> Everything that is absorbed and registered in your mind adds to the collection of ideas stored in the memory: a sort of library that you can consult whenever a problem arises. So, essentially the more you have seen, experienced and absorbed, the more points of reference you will have to help you decide which direction to take: your frame of reference expands.
>
> Herman Hertzberger, *Lessons for Students in Architecture* (1991)

A designerly way of knowing

Having studied design knowledge through drawings, from interactions with computers, and through conversations, we are now ready to attempt some more general understanding of what constitutes design knowledge. The quotation at the top of the first chapter in this book comes from Nigel Cross's paper of the same name (Cross, 1982). He uses the delightful phrase 'a designerly way of knowing'. It suggests both that there may be more than one way of knowing and that some may be more useful than others to designers. This is a phenomenon that those involved in design education are all too familiar with. It has long been recognized, for example, that there are real difficulties in teaching some of the more technical and theoretical subjects in the curriculum of design degrees. For example, student architects can be taught how to calculate the sizes of the main structural members of buildings, or they can be shown how to estimate the energy consumption of their designs. Indeed they can be taught such subjects well enough for them to pass examinations which form part of their degree courses. However, when their tutors look for the impact of this knowledge on their studio design work it may be less apparent. To get those students to go one step further and use this knowledge to generate more innovative structures or sustainable buildings may be quite another matter. Of course some designers have managed this and we have seen the work of Santiago Calatrava and Ken Yeang respectively in this book who are both enormously creative in these two areas.

Why should this be? How is it that knowledge may be gained and retained and yet apparently remain unusable in the design process? At least part of the answer to this question seems to lie in the nature of knowledge that designers collect and manipulate and the kind of memory in which they store it.

Precedent

Designers commonly and frequently make great use of what they often refer to as 'precedent'. Precedents are often either whole or partial pieces of designs that the designer is aware of. They may be previously employed solutions by the same designer, by famous designers, buildings, landscapes or towns seen on study visits or even on holiday. Today, very frequently these precedents will not have been experienced live, but through images in magazines, journals, books, on the Internet or television. Perhaps the furniture, clothes or possessions of characters in films may be used. In previous times before the introduction of the digital image, designers relied heavily on photographs and before that on drawings. But before the introduction of photography and modern methods of reproduction travel was essential in the education of a young designer who would be expected to take the grand tour to build up this knowledge.

Precedent is such a vital, central and crucial feature of the design process that it plays a central role in all design education. One of the key objectives of design education is to expose young students to a veritable barrage of images and experiences upon which they can draw later for precedent. A further objective is to inculcate an attitude of respect for gathering precedent and to develop the skills to do so. Young students of design everywhere are exhorted to keep sketchbooks and to learn to draw to record what they see. In Chapter 4 on designing by drawing we saw examples of this in what we called 'experiential' drawings.

Precedent versus reference

Precedent can most simply be understood in relation to the practice of law where it is commonly used for debate and argument. Lawyers will use their knowledge and ability to analyse legal situations to search for aspects of previous cases that might be similar enough to count as precedents. Of course some of the ensuing legal argument may revolve around whether this claimed precedent is sufficiently similar to guide thinking and outcome in the current case. Goldschmidt (1998) has argued that design precedent is different in this respect. In fact of course no two design situations are ever identical, and Goldschmidt points out that this is not necessary for precedent to be useful for a designer. In fact unlike the lawyer, the designer is not trying to demonstrate a close parallel with the precedent but is rather using something that is sufficiently similar in some respects to become a useful point of departure. Goldschmidt therefore argues persuasively that the term 'precedent' is less satisfactory than the term 'reference' as a generic description of this phenomenon in design. In fact she prefers to see precedents as a subclass of the more general idea of reference. While in principle she is right, the term precedent seems to have become common parlance in many practising and professional design circles so we will continue to use it here.

Solution-based precedent

In fact the idea of precedent almost in its legal sense has also been used in design. Going right back as far as Palladio, architects have made extensive use of the pattern book. In 1728 James Gibb presented his *Book of Architecture* which he described as 'for the use of gentlemen who might be concerned in building, especially in remote parts of the country'. Clearly the pattern book represented an important way of communicating precedent before electronic communication and easy international travel. Later when writing his authoritative treatise on Georgian architecture, Dan Cruickshank was to observe that such pattern books were so effective that they largely eliminated regional variations in style and detail (Cruickshank and Wyld, 1975). Greek revival patterns also became very fashionable in the UK and the Victorians seemed to have a positive passion for pattern books of housing. In the early colonial days of the modern USA, the colonial architectural style and in particular housing plans and elevations were found in a proliferation of pattern books.

Perhaps the early modern movement, as Goldschmidt also observes, was a period in which precedent played an unusually minor role in what was thought to be a logical functionalist process. Design students were taught that the modern movement was not just another style but a full stop at the end of history and represented a fundamental and irreversible change in design values. This position is articulated by Christopher Alexander (1964) in his famous and seminal treatise on *Notes on the Synthesis of Form* which we briefly studied in Chapter 2:

> If the pattern of the problems could only be seen as it is and not as the bromide image of a previous solution conveniently at hand in the catalogue or magazine around the corner.

In other words 'stop being solution focused and become problem focused'! Well this appeal to use logical procedures is entirely understandable in the absence of what we have learned since about the psychology of how designers actually think and why. We have seen repeatedly in this book evidence that designers use a much more solution focused approach than scientists, and that argument has been made in more detail elsewhere (Lawson, 1979). We have seen that it is the very nature of design problems that makes such a strategy sensible. Such empirical work and the consequent analysis were not available to Alexander and his plea to logic was even more understandable in the cultural climate of the time in which it was written. Alexander tried to engineer such a change with his famous mathematical way of analysing design problems in order to deconstruct them into simple subcomponents each of which could be solved in a functionalist manner. The rest of the process then became one of recombining those subsolutions. Nearly half a century later we can see that his techniques have hardly ever been applied in practice.

Indeed the post-modern world of design has rejected such a view and it is now fashionable again explicitly to call on historical styles, although frequently in a fragmentary form. Pattern books have continued to exist though mainly for the user and consumer rather than the professional designer. In the period immediately after the Second World War, pattern books for fashion designs were extremely popular particularly in Europe. As money was short and manufacturing slow to recover it was common for the population to make its own clothes copying and adapting designs from pattern books that were available in shops. More recently the newly found popularity of the television 'make-over' programmes for interiors and gardens has given rise to pattern books for people to use to re-fashion their properties.

Christopher Alexander and his many collaborators (1977) have produced a series of books that appear to be diametrically opposed in their view of problems and solutions to his earlier position. This series has in fact culminated in a title, *A Pattern Language*, that would have seemed inconceivable at the height of the modern movement. Here Alexander and his collaborators tell us that: 'We have tried in each solution to capture the invariant property common to all places which succeed in solving the problem.' In other words Alexander is no longer exhorting designers to see problems themselves in the abstract way he called for in his earlier work but is instead recommending that they study good working solutions. Alexander's earlier criticism of designers for their dependence on precedent as provided through photographs in magazines had by then largely fallen on deaf ears and the magazines have continued to be published and remain popular. Theoreticians it seems cannot change practice simply by rhetoric. If a large body of people behave consistently over a substantial period of time then a good working hypothesis is usually that they have collectively adapted sensibly to their situation. All this provides fairly good evidence to support the view that precedent is seen by designers as an important part of their knowledge upon which they are able to draw in a 'designerly way'. It is therefore certainly worth our attention here.

A key and defining characteristic of design precedents, however, must surely lie in the fact that they are whole or partial solutions. That is to say they demonstrate possible ways of doing things in design. The use of precedent by the architects of today is much less comprehensive than in the past hence the strength of Goldschmidt's argument. Pattern books may exist for the consumer but they are not a significant force in professional design. Instead architects of today make use of precedents that are partial rather than complete designs. What problems that they solve are not necessarily identified, are seldom recorded, and are hardly ever analysed. In essence they offer answers or part answer to questions that are seldom explicitly stated.

In many fields of knowledge this would seem a curious if not rather questionable way of proceeding. Such knowledge may well be thought of outside design as of rather doubtful value. And yet throughout the history of professional design we have seen such knowledge plays an important if not central role in the process.

Types of precedent

Clothing design has long been heavily influenced by precedent and in English the word fashion refers both to this field of design and to a temporary trend. Fashion design it seems is heavily influenced by what other people have been doing very recently. But also here often explicitly new designs are seen to be based on previous sets of ideas that have been literally 'out of fashion' for a while. Indeed it almost seems a prerequisite that a certain amount of time has passed and that several other cycles of change have taken place before a set of design ideas can come back into fashion again. The idea of revival is not new in design nor is it limited to the world of fashion. Architecture was once dominated by the revival or resuscitation of design ideas from the ancient world. Egyptian, Greek and Roman styles have all had their periods of revival. The Victorians even loved the Gothic. Although these cycles were much longer than in the modern world, and certainly in the modern world of fashion, they can still be seen to be a very similar phenomenon of great enthusiasms that wear off in time.

The modern movement in design, however, seemed to put an end to such nonsense, as it was portrayed by the functionalists. Mere fashion or style was no longer seen as serious. The functionalists really only in the end introduced another form of precedent which has outlived their historical period. They depended on the precedent of typology. To this day an architectural library or bookshop will devote much of its shelves to studies of buildings by function or type. Schools, housing, airports, hospitals, law courts, theatres and any number of other significant types will be studied and most of these treatises are dominated by illustrations of solutions.

Recently we have also seen the rise of the signature designer. Famous designers, whether they be in fashion such as Vivienne Westwood, in product design such as Philipe Starck, in furniture design such as Marcel Breuer, or architecture such Norman Foster, have attracted so much attention that they have become the subject of numerous books and articles. While there are theoretical and philosophical debates to be found in this literature it remains dominated by the design output of these star designers. Other evidence of this can be seen very graphically in our libraries and bookshops that devote much shelf space to such books. A simple study of one university architecture library and one specialist design bookshop revealed that over 50 per cent of their book stacks were accounted for by typological and designer books while by comparison less than 5 per cent were devoted to the subject of this book, the design process itself!

In fact we can see that design references or precedents can cover many different aspects of design problems. In *How Designers Think* I presented a three-dimensional model of design constraints that can be used to map out the structure of design problems (Lawson, 1997). One dimension of this model describes the range of types of problems. The typological material we have just discussed corresponds to the 'radical' constraints layer of that dimension. The vast majority of the use of historical styles offers rules that correspond to the 'formal' or compositional and sometimes the 'symbolic' constraint layers. Another dimension of the model shows the sources of design problems that we discussed in Chapter 3 of this book. The copying of individual designer styles clearly corresponds to the 'designer generated' constraints layer. I showed that in the office of the architect John Outram all the staff have to learn to speak the design language of the practice. Outram is quite explicit about this (Lawson, 1994): 'The longer they stay the more adept they get. If they refuse to speak it at all then there is a mutual parting, as it were.' In fact the Outram language is in turn highly sophisticated, intensely symbolic and hugely dependent on the study of precedent.

Design data handbooks have been developed since the advent of functionalism. These are not pattern books in the sense of offering complete designs. Nor are they guides to whole buildings of a particular typology. Instead they offer fragments of prototypical designs that are recognized as good practice. The *AJ Metric Handbook*, for example, provides architects with a range of fragments of designs that might come in handy. For example, they include arrangements of seats and tables in restaurants, library reading rooms or lecture theatres. Ways of arranging car parking spaces and fragments of vehicle access and servicing arrangements are listed. Sample staircases, arranging the work surfaces in domestic kitchens, fragments of bathrooms, public toilets and other such spaces are all shown. Industrial designers are similarly provided for with anthropometric and ergonomic source data presented in partial solution form.

Using precedent

All this discussion so far begs a very difficult and yet important question. The question is exactly how do designers make use of precedent when they are actually thinking about a new design project? Donald Schön (1988) attempts some answers to this in his study of what he calls 'rules, types and worlds'. Schön argues that designers 'tend to treat each design situation as a unique universe of one'. If this is correct, and it certainly chimes with all our experience of the modern process, how can that be reconciled with the idea of precedent? This is of course exactly why design precedents are not like legal ones, and thus Goldschmidt's argument in favour of using the term 'reference' (Goldschmidt, 1998). Schön introduces that idea that designers 'inhabit' what he calls 'worlds' which he describes as containing 'particular configurations of things, relations and qualities'. For Schön then these worlds are used to contain design knowledge in structures that make it usable when actually designing.

Episodic memory and design knowledge

At the end of the previous chapter we left an argument hanging about the importance of memory and its role in understanding design thinking. We are now ready to pick that argument up again. We are used to the distinction between short- and long-term memory. Short-term memory is by definition used to remember information for relatively short periods of time, like looking up a telephone number in the directory. It is generally recognized to fade rapidly and have very limited capacity, in fact about seven items can be stored reliably (Miller, 1956). Long-term memory by comparison is thought to be capable of lasting a lifetime, and to have unlimited capacity under normal conditions. Now it is important to draw a further distinction between the long-term memory types of theoretical and experiential memory. These two types of memory are more often described as 'semantic' and 'episodic' in the cognitive psychology literature (Tulving, 1983). First, let us see how they are different and conduct some simple experiments that will enable you to prove this for yourself.

You may remember many events in your life. In fact you put little or no effort into this form of remembering. To be more correct, you may put no effort at all into storing the information but you may later struggle to recall it. However often once reminded, you may remember relatively clearly events that you had no intention specifically to store away for future recall. Imagine you meet an old friend for the first time in many years. The likelihood is that your conversation will centre on reminiscence. Your friend might say something like 'do you remember when we went to ...'. You might indeed recall this and say, 'yes of course, and there was a tremendous storm that afternoon'. Your friend might reply 'oh yes so there was, I had quite forgotten that!' Such a conversation is quite imaginable and readily demonstrates the nature of effortless storage and sometimes free and sometimes difficult recall.

By contrast to this 'experiential' memory, you will also probably have had to study for some examinations. You will have been required to remember theories and related ideas perhaps even formulae and procedures. You may have found all this very difficult to remember and had to work very hard to store the knowledge. For example, you may recall trying to remember dates for a history exam or formulae for a science exam. This is of course not a memory of an event or an experience but of some semantic theoretical structure, or a set of rules. Such information is generally abstract and thus unsuitable for the symbolic, schemata-based long-term memory. You may have used some devices to try to make such abstract information 'real' or meaningful in order to store it more easily. My mother would always rehearse a little poem she had learned as a child in order to recall how many days there are in each month. There are similar examples to be found in the school child's world for remembering the kings and queens of England, the various fates which befell the wives of Henry VIII, the order of elements in the periodic table and so on.

I have an even more dramatic personal example I use to illustrate this difference between semantic and episodic memory. A long time ago when I was student of architecture at Oxford they expected us to be able to draw from memory most of the famous buildings of history. Indeed this was essential if we wanted to pass our history exams. We got up to all sorts of clever devices for remembering particular building plans and elevations. Unfortunately since I have not used this knowledge for many years I have largely forgotten it. However, I can very clearly remember the pain of study. One building in particular that caused us difficulty was Haghia Sophia in Istanbul which has both a ground plan and an upper walls and domes plan that relate in a complex manner (Fig.8.1). I know it involved a clever aggregation of circles and squares but that is the extent of my recall of the actual formula. In fact I had to devise the formula all over again in order to produce the illustration here (Fig. 8.2). But I can still very easily recall the event of drawing up the original rules which proved adequate in enabling us to pass our history exams. In fact I recall a particular day sat having a picnic lunch in Christchurch Meadow next to the college where I was living rehearsing with two other students how to draw these particular plans (Fig. 8.3). I even remember the weather, some details of what we ate for lunch and that we went on the river in the afternoon. Thus the

Figure 8.1
Haghia Sophia in Istanbul

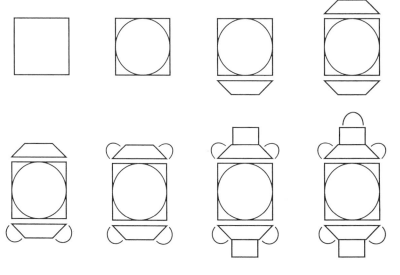

Figure 8.2
A set of progressive rules for establishing the plan of the upper walls and domes of Haghia Sophia

formulae for generating plans, which were theoretical, have faded even though I studied them very hard at the time. However, the experience of devising them I still recall even though I made no attempt whatever to store or remember it! In fact although the semantic memory has totally failed me the episodic memory is remarkably detailed.

Another way of demonstrating the distinction is to try to recall your own earliest experiential memory. You will find it hard to know what it was but you can be fairly sure that you have little recall from very early childhood. However, you were learning language and remembering it quite clearly even before your earliest experiential memory. Similarly we find that people can suffer extreme forms of amnesia so that they are quite unable to recall periods of their life. But they may still remember, and be able to use language, and in

Figure 8.3
Almost exactly where I remember sitting to develop the forgotten rules from Fig. 8.2

many cases use sophisticated professional theoretical knowledge. I had a close relative who suffered horribly with episodic memory loss in later life and would not be able to remember the events of the previous day or even hour. Yet she could clearly recall some recipes that she had not cooked for many years and recite or sing without error the words of her favourite hymns! These are common characteristics of this terrible affliction.

Theoretical or semantic memory is stored and recalled in a way different from experiential or episodic memory. The fact is the two systems seem remarkably independent. Sadly psychologists know far more about short-term memory and semantic memory than they do about long-term episodic memory. This is most probably something to do with their relationship with laboratory work as opposed to fieldwork. It is much easier to do experiments under controlled laboratory conditions using memory tests lasting a few minutes than it is to check memory performance over many years in normal life. Perhaps this is one reason why some aspects of design knowledge have also been neglected in design research and theory.

Design precedent and episodic memory

Of course all this material that we have been discussing here in the form of precedent or reference is stored through episodic memory. We remember designs we have seen either in real life or in magazines. There is little or no theoretical way of storing this knowledge, and indeed it is hard to see how there ever can be and yet retain the flexibility of recall that is so characteristic of creative designers.

So how do designers make use of this episodic knowledge based on precedent or reference? If we return to the parallel with the law, then we can see that a skilled lawyer will have the ability to analyse and develop an argument that shows the parallel between the current situation and the claimed precedent. But how is the precedent found in the first place? Well here our parallel with design begins again to let us down. Today's legal library is very dependent on digital search procedures that require legal cases to be classified and catalogued. Goldschmidt (1998) calls for the development of a classification system for design references. She claims the development of information science and computing technology should now be capable 'both in terms of storage capacities and in terms of multiple indexing that allows many retrieval routines and associational connections'. She may be right, although she deliberately does not attempt any further development of the idea herself. However, it is hard to see designers ever being able to agree on some universal cataloguing system for design references. Surely one of the unique selling points of human designers is their ability to break the mould as it were and develop their own unusual cross-references that others may not have seen before. In fact the general direction of information science is taking us away from systems of predefined cataloguing and towards heuristic search engines. The idea of the database that has limited slots into which to put knowledge is increasingly seen as inflexible and out of date. In this sense computational techniques may be moving in the right direction. At this stage it is difficult to know whether Goldschmidt is right and we can really develop sufficiently good search engines to compete with the creative human mind.

For now at least designers will have to continue relying largely on their own experience just as lawyers previously did and probably still frequently do. In fact there is considerable evidence that the build-up of experience is one of the factors that distinguishes experts in a field from their more humble counterparts. We can now already suggest two components that might be necessary in acquiring this expert status. First there might be the process of acquiring a very large pool of experience, and second, the ability to access this in flexible ways. These themes will be explored more fully in the next chapter.

Design education

This book is not specifically about the education of designers but of course it is intended to help in that process. As we saw at the beginning of this chapter, it is quite possible to teach design students some technical or theoretical subjects in such a way that they acquire knowledge but appear to show little or no understanding or appreciation of this when they design. For example, architects can be taught about building science and pass their examination with flying colours and yet their design projects show little evidence of exploiting this knowledge and they continue to design buildings that are environmentally inefficient and uncomfortable. Building construction is another subject that is notoriously vulnerable to this phenomenon in schools of architecture. Similarly the teaching of history or philosophy of design may leave students with well-developed knowledge that they nevertheless find hard to connect with the knowledge they use when actually designing.

The real problem here seems to be that this knowledge has been taught in such a way that it is not 'designerly', to reuse Nigel Cross's delightful phrase.

In fact if it is taught as largely theoretical or semantic knowledge it will be stored differently from the experiential or episodic knowledge upon which students depend for establishing their precedent. As we have seen, designers work in the solution focused manner that depends heavily upon design gambits based upon recognizing design situations amenable to solving certain problem situations. If students are establishing this pattern of working then they may find it very difficult to connect and use theoretical knowledge presented in lecture theatres when actually designing.

We have also made reference here to bookshops and libraries. It is worth noting that the library for the design subjects in a university often looks quite different to the library for most other subjects. This is of course because the students in design need access to large amounts of experiential knowledge to help them form precedent to use in ways that cannot be predicted and filed away in some referencing system. One university librarian argued with me about the nature of the architecture library by claiming that those students hardly used the library at all. The figures he relied upon were of book loans. Of course he had no figures representing the number of times design students came into the library, scanned though dozens of books and journals and left without borrowing a book to take home and read. Only recently I have struggled to explain to my own university library how absurd it is to think of separating out what they see as undergraduate and post-graduate texts into different buildings. This may work for many academic subjects but not for design. The nature of design knowledge means it just is not like that. A post-graduate student does not know different knowledge to an undergraduate. But this is getting us very close to the interesting question of expert knowledge in design and that is the subject of the next chapter.

Expert knowledge in design

It took me forty years to find a way to have this communication of my brain and my paper ... and I feel I am now quite eloquent in my way of doing it.

Herman Hertzberger

Vernacular in the sense that each time you come to the problem you already have large elements of the solution. It's vernacular in the sense of process rather than product.

Richard MacCormac

Genius is one per cent inspiration and ninety-nine per cent perspiration.

Thomas Alva Edison

Are there various levels of expertise which we can identify among designers? In what ways are novices or student designers less expert than more experienced practitioners? These are questions that remain difficult to answer for a number of reasons. Not least among these reasons is a rather intractable difficulty in research methodology. A considerable amount of our current knowledge about the design process derives from experiments in which the subjects are put under some controlled conditions rather than simply observed in practice. The most commonly available subjects for such experiments are often quite inexperienced designers and even students.

By contrast it is not easy to get experienced and expert designers to be the subjects of detailed experiments. There are probably several reasons for this. They are simply too busy to find the time to take part in design experiments. They have very little to gain in exposing their methods and potentially something to lose. This loss might be thought to be in giving away secrets, but equally it could be in the loss of the mystique that has tended to surround signature designers over the last couple of decades.

To learn more about design expertise we may have to use a variety of techniques. First, to examine the very best designers' processes we might need to use different research methods such as interviews and real-time observation. Second, we may study rather less successful but nonetheless experienced designers under more controlled conditions and compare them with very immature students to discover any patterns in development that may be discernible. Third, we might compare design students on long courses such as architecture in which we can see substantial development over perhaps five years or so. Finally, we can see what we might learn from studies of expertise in other related fields of cognitive activity. All these techniques have been used and from such studies we can now begin to build up a picture of what expert designers seem to know that novices may not. However, it remains difficult directly to compare the processes of truly outstanding designers with their much less illustrious counterparts since most researchers have tended to use different methods of investigation.

But let us begin at the beginning. So far in this book we have seen a number of clues about what designers know, how they acquire that knowledge and the impact it makes in the design process. But there are also many issues we have not discussed here that might make up the total expertise required by a top designer. They will have to acquire a great deal of technical knowledge about the nature and performance of the materials, components and systems they construct their design from. We might call this 'practical' knowledge. In the previous chapter we saw how designers acquire knowledge of a typological kind. An architect specializing in school design clearly has specialized knowledge about schools. A product designer producing cutlery is likely to acquire quite different sets of both practical and typological knowledge.

Levels of expertise

To understand expertise in design we must first explore the idea of expertise itself. Kees Dorst (2003) maps out five levels of expertise although he acknowledges the influence on his taxonomy of discussions with Hubert Dreyfus. The significance of these five levels is not just that they represent an ascending order of expertise but they also correspond with five ways of perceiving. Dorst calls the levels 'novice', 'beginner', 'competent', 'proficient' and 'expert'. According to Dorst (and Dreyfus) the novice tends to follow strict rules as laid down probably from instruction, but also tends mainly to consider the 'objective features of a situation'. The beginner has moved on slightly and is more sensitive to the situational context and more aware of exceptions to rules. The competent problem solver, however, works in a substantively different way being much more selective as to which problem features to attend to and having much more clearly articulated plans of working. At this level of expertise there is more seeking out opportunities and more willingness to use trial and error based on past experience. There is therefore more learning and reflection involved at this level. The proficient problem solver has therefore acquired enough of this experience and reflection to accurately recognize important features and make appropriate plans on a frequent basis. The expert recognizes the nature of the situation intuitively and performs appropriate actions without the need for conscious mental effort. This multi-stage acquisition of expertise seems to make sense when one examines the way students of design appear to learn. Their progress often appears not to be steady but to be a series of plateaux connected by apparently significant epiphanies. So how is this development of expertise manifest in the acquisition of expertise, specifically in design?

Development of schemata

The first stage of the development of some expertise probably precedes the actual acquisition of knowledge and indeed is substantially necessary before much useful knowledge can be accumulated. This is the stage of concept formation or the development of design schemata. In fact of course we all have schemata or concepts about designed objects, but for most people these remain largely superficial and few in number. For the professional designer, however, these schemata become both more numerous and more sophisticated. This is both inevitable and necessary but often surprisingly deals with information that is also apparent to ordinary users of design. A brick wall may look to be just that to an ordinary passer-by. However, to an architect who has studied such things the bricks have a size, shape, colour, and surface finish which may be identified by name. The pattern of laying the bricks in the wall is known as bonding. This is itself of course a schema. However, it has many possible instantiations such as 'stretcher', 'header', 'English', 'Flemish', 'garden wall' and so on. In addition the way of finishing the mortar joint may be identified as 'bucket handle', 'flush', 'struck', 'recessed' and so on. Thus while the passer-by and the architect both see the same wall the architect 'knows' about it quite differently and can differentiate brick walls more elaborately and infer more information from them. For example, the knowledgeable will be aware that Dutch and English bricks traditionally have different proportions. One of the paradoxes of architecture is that architects have such special knowledge about buildings that they can hardly perceive them at all in the way the users they design for do!

Of course we all acquire such schemata often without apparent effort and without noticing that we have done so, whereas the professional designer will study to acquire these concepts and is likely to have had to pass examinations to demonstrate a certain level of familiarity with the schemata and proficiency at manipulating the concepts related to them. A delightful example of this process can be seen in the illustration, kindly but of course totally unintentionally, provided by my daughter when very young indeed (Fig. 9.1). The drawing is of the university building where I work and she completed it while waiting for me to come out of a meeting one day. She was coming into the university with me while her mother was unexpectedly in hospital giving birth to her brother. We live in a house in a village with a large garden in which she played as a child. Driving into the city my daughter would ask about the tall blocks of flats we passed and was clearly puzzled as to how their occupants managed without gardens and where the front doors were for the flats on the higher levels. Clearly my answers to these questions, while simultaneously negotiating the rush hour traffic, were less than adequate as each answer yielded yet another question about a building typology for which she had no usable schemata. Our university building is similarly tall and has an internal vertical moving car 'paternoster' system for shifting people between floors as well as conventional lifts, both of which puzzled her greatly at the time (Fig. 9.2). So when I went into my meeting she sat down to draw the building but could only do so based on the limited architectural schemata available to her, all largely based on housing. The results are therefore totally understandable once

Figure 9.1
A drawing derived from the architectural knowledge of a very young child (see also in colour on front cover)

you appreciate that she was drawing not what she had seen, but what she 'knew' must be there by relying on these limited schemata. The pitched roof on the top of the building is an obvious example of this. Note though how sophisticated is the understanding of symmetry and axial emphasis revealed by the need to place the door in the middle of each little house, and indeed the door knocker in the middle of the door. More careful examination will also reveal knockers on the lift doors and 'strings' emerging from their tops to represent some mechanism by which they might by lifted up the building.

Hopefully students of architecture quickly acquire more sophisticated and numerous architectural schemata once they begin their period of higher education. This process will continue as they become professional architects and work in practice. The idea of the formation of schemata was introduced in Chapter 7 on design conversations. It was through the study of conversations that we recognized the need for shared ideas based on concepts or schemata. We saw how the conversations in Richard MacCormac's design office relied upon schemata such as 'belvedere', and the 'vessel' that was to become the central idea in the chapel at Fitzwilliam College, Cambridge. During an interview

Figure 9.2
The same building

with MacCormac himself he was describing to me the process by which this design came into being:

> at some stage the thing [the worship space] became sort of round but I can't remember how ... early on we were playing with round shapes in square containers, you know the sort of thing.

Here Richard was obviously expecting that I would understand from this reference a whole series of architectural ideas, and that I would recognize the architectural game being played. I remember him looking at my eyes to see if this was the case. He must have inferred that it was or I guess the conversation would have halted or proceeded differently. In fact the conversation would have been almost impossible since a huge quantity of knowledge about the repertoire of geometric tricks commonly understood by architects would have been missing and the subsequent phases of the discussion assumed this was understood.

Listening to conversation in such practices reveals just how extraordinarily efficient communication becomes since enormously complex and sophisticated sets of ideas can be referred to using simple diagrams, catchphrases (for example, 'round shapes in square containers') or even single words (for example, 'belvedere'). Such a phenomenon is hardly new to us. It is precisely that of concept formation or the development of schemata. For experienced architects the concept or schema of 'round shapes in square containers' includes not just the simple idea of that geometry but the whole game of contrasting the curved and straight lines, and all the examples and variations have been developed by other architects. For MacCormac's practice members, the schema of 'belvedere' was not restricted to the commonly shared idea of a viewing tower. For them it was not a matter of a building typology at all but rather a whole series of devices for organizing space vertically in order to afford dramatic views that helped building users to build mental maps of their surroundings. They collectively delight in these ideas and have studied them and exploited them in previous designs.

In Chapter 5 we saw the experiments done by one of my research students Alexandre Menezes, in which he asked students of architecture to describe drawings to other students who would then have to reproduce the drawing as accurately as they could from this description. We saw that the results from these ingenious studies generally support the work of Bartlett who showed how long-term memory is dependent on the development of schemata. In the case of Menezes' experiment on design students the results tend to show that the more experienced students had acquired more schemata about design and relied more upon these when describing the architectural drawing.

In general then the first stage of the acquisition of expertise in design seems to depend heavily on the development of concepts or schemata commonly used in the design domain and likely to be shared by other designers.

Acquisition of precedent

The next stage of acquisition of expertise must surely be that of the development of a substantial body of experiential or episodic knowledge potentially useful in designing. We explored these ideas in the previous chapter which showed just how important such knowledge is in designing compared with entirely theoretical knowledge. Of course the process of schemata formation and development continues as this knowledge is acquired. There is a two-way interactive process at work here with which cognitive and educational psychology is entirely familiar.

This acquisition of the pool of precedent upon which a designer can draw obviously begins during education. In fact design educators seem to take on the task not only of beginning to expose their students to a great deal of what they judge to be valuable precedent, but they also encourage the development of the practice of absorbing precedent. The first of these two is evident in a number of ways in design schools. The reliance on field trips, the heavy use of graphical representation, and the organization of libraries all offer this evidence.

Design schools commonly organize substantial numbers of field trips to museums, galleries, buildings and places. During these trips students are not only shown material but encouraged to sketch and record. No school of design could possibly be effective without methods of reproducing and displaying images of design situations.

The libraries that support such schools are full of such images. As we saw in the previous chapter, the way students of design use their libraries is quite different from the way many students of many other subjects do. This often causes confusion and misunderstanding at universities that try to operate campus-wide library provision. Designers need their libraries close at hand to their studios, may actually borrow fewer books, but may use them more intensively in browsing for ideas. A common misunderstanding among university librarians is that design students make little use of libraries. One librarian actually argued this to me once on the basis of figures he had collected for the number of loans taken out by students from different faculties. Design students may relatively rarely borrow books compared to their academic peers in other subject areas, but they may by contrast spend far more time browsing for precedent. Perhaps the law library with its case histories offers a similar pattern though with its lack of visual imagery may not appear to. This further compounds the misunderstanding that librarians and other academics have about design students. Not only do they not very often take books out to read, but when they are in the library they spend a lot of their time just looking at the pictures! This cannot be serious study surely! Well yes it is very serious. It is one of the central ways in which designers use knowledge. It is at the heart of the process of acquiring useful precedent.

Development of guiding principles

In *Design in Mind* I studied the design processes of a selection of highly successful architects (Lawson, 1994). In that study it became apparent that their processes had many common features but that each was also unique. The one factor which was identified in every single case was the presence and role of what I described as 'guiding principles'. These 'guiding principles' are sets of ideas, beliefs and values that operate for the designer spanning many projects rather than just one and in most cases develop in a coherent way over their career. Taken together these principles represent an intellectual programme which appears to have a very strong influence on individual projects but more fundamentally appears to be at the root of the satisfaction these designers take from their work. In many cases the designers studied actually write about their guiding principles, while in other cases critics and biographers do this job.

I have since argued that it is the existence of these ideas that allows us to see design as a form of research (Lawson, 2002b). In *How Designers Think* I have shown how in the case of more experienced designers these 'guiding principles' are often the source of what Jane Darke called the 'primary generator' in a design project (Lawson, 1997). In Donald Schön's terms we can see these 'guiding principles' as the source of the 'frames' they apply in the project (Schön, 1983). We can see therefore a two-way interaction here. In each project the 'guiding principles' are brought to bear and give the problem structure and direct the framing of the situation. However, the knowledge gained in each project further enhances the understanding of the 'guiding principles' which become more developed, elaborate and clearly articulated as a result. An example would be the work of the Malaysian architect Ken Yeang. Ken's 'guiding principles' are clearly about how to design high rise architecture in the climate of the wet tropical countries such as his own, and from this how to develop a sense of regionalism. When I first studied Ken Yeang he showed me a document that he gave to all new members of staff coming to join the practice. Later he published a book, and gradually that book has grown into many other publications all articulating the ideas behind his design work as a coherent set of principles.

Thus a higher level of expertise in design seems to be associated with the development of a set of 'guiding principles' that transcend any one project. These principles represent not only the ideals and values of the designer but a growing and authoritative body of knowledge about how to realize those principles through design. In turn this set of principles is clearly framing the development of precedent. These principles appear to act as a major filter which in turn permits the selection of material for the body of precedent gathered and used by the designer and his or her practice. This can be seen as a largely self-supporting and self-reinforcing process inexorably driving the designer towards something that others may see as a style, but which all the designers I have studied claim to be far more profound than the stylistic issues often taking centre stage in the writings of design critics.

Ability of recognition

However, it seems that high level expertise can demonstrate further stages of cognitive development that turn out to have enormous significance for the way designers think. It seems that those who are often seen as experts do relatively little analytical thinking. Their experience enables such 'experts' to recognize almost without analysis the features of well-established precedents in the current case. De Groot (1965) argued that chess masters were able to recognize complete situations during play and from their previous study of them have ready ideas on how they might respond.

There is little empirical investigation of this phenomenon in the design field, but two pieces of anecdotal evidence might be helpful. In Chapter 5 on designing with drawings we saw that many expert designers seem to like working on small drawings. In fact we quoted Herman Hertzberger's own explanation of this as being like playing chess and his horror at the idea of playing chess on one of those huge outdoor boards. The board around the corner from his office (Fig. 9.3) probably made him think of the parallel. It is certainly not easy to take in the whole board and recognize a particular pattern.

De Groot's work showed that chess masters could remember mid-game board situations much more reliably than novices. However, their comparative expertise vanished when asked to remember randomly positioned pieces that did not relate to game situations. Taken together these results suggest something we are familiar with in design, the use of known precedents that have been studied and about which the expert has schemata. These precedents linked problem to solution and such chess masters could articulate this link. Thus the schema for the situation also includes one or more known gambits for solving it.

So we may conclude from this work that when grand master chess players look at a board situation they do not apprehend the pattern entirely geometrically but rather at least in part symbolically. It is perhaps also similar to the

Figure 9.3
When playing on these outdoor chess boards it is hard to see the whole game at a glance

process that appears to take place when an experienced user of a language reads speedily from a book. Here the evidence suggests we do not construct words by reading every letter, piecing them together and arriving at the word as if one were using a dictionary. If this were so it would of course be impossible for those of us who remain bad spellers to continue to read accurately and reliably appreciate meaning. We have other evidence from experiments on short-term memory. Such work has shown that we have a relatively small capacity to remember items presented apparently independently of symbolic content for short periods. This would include looking up numbers in the telephone directory, for example. Such experiments have shown that seven items is our normal maximum reliable capacity here. Thus you will find it very hard to remember sequences of letters in excess of seven long. However, if those letters are reorganized into words you may remember sequences of up to seven words accurately. If those words are reorganized into well-known sayings, poems or songs you may remember the names of up to seven songs accurately. From these you might reconstruct the words of each song, and the sequences of letters that constitute them. Remembering and recalling such a lengthy sequence of letters, however, would have been totally beyond your abilities. This has led us to appreciate the distinction between long- and short-term memory and their relative dependence on formal and symbolic content. From this we are also able to understand a great deal about the way the designed world is perceived and structured, but that is another argument (Lawson, 2001).

For our purposes here, however, we are more interested in how designers come to recognize problem situations. It seems highly likely that this is at least in part done by recognizing possible solutions to them. It is not just that the more experienced designer has seen more problems than the novice but that he or she has seen many more solutions too. We have seen that the presentation of design information is dominated by representations or portrayals of solutions whether in the flesh as it were of the real objects or in the pictures of them in magazines and books. Sometimes, but not always, such representations are accompanied by descriptive analytical text which may relate the solution to the problem. This is most typically the case in, for example, books about design solution typologies such as housing or airports.

It seems likely then that to some extent at least the experienced designer is interacting with the problem situation by recognizing in some way possible solutions rather than by recognizing the problem directly. There are some clues as to how this might work from research into expertise in other areas. More recent research on chess playing has shown that expert players break the board down into segments or chunks such as attack and defence, and can remember larger chunks than can novice players (Chase and Simon, 1973). Similarly expert computer programmers appear to recall larger chunks of code and to be more able to adapt them to their current situation (Adelson, 1981). Chi *et al.* (1981) compared experts and novices solving problems in physics and found that they used quite different methods of classifying problems. Novices tended to group together problems that had similar superficial characteristics, whereas experts grouped together problems that were amenable to solution by the same principles. We also know that the one common and most widely used tool for designing is that of sketching solutions. We further know that designers adopt solution focused rather than predominantly problem focused cognitive strategies. Taken together all this makes sense. Designers sketch possible solutions or fragments of solutions or characteristics of solutions. As Schön would say 'they have a conversation' with such drawings and from this conversation recognize possibilities from their pool of stored precedent or reference material.

Design gambits

Chess masters are able to play demonstration matches where they take on many amateur players simultaneously moving from board to board. If they were relying upon analysis of each board as they came to it this would take too long, but using recognition they are able to use a standard gambit and pass on to the next game. There is a further interesting analogy for us here. Chess masters can easily defeat amateurs in such a way. However, to beat another chess master who is also recognizing the situation and similarly has a vast pool of precedent and gambits to rely on, they need to create something new, original and surprising. This sounds remarkably like what we also expect from expert designers. We expect them not just to solve problems well, but to surprise us and add something new to the pool of precedent that in turn other designers rely upon.

The architect Richard MacCormac described his practice as 'having a repertoire of tricks'. These can be seen as design gambits or possible ways of solving recognizable problems. Of course these are often based on the guiding principles that we discussed earlier. In Richard MacCormac's case those are often to do with light and geometry: 'We look for a clear geometric analogy for the content of the problem.' Further examination then reveals that MacCormac has many geometric precedents that he relies on. These 'tricks' or gambits are actually patterns known to have certain properties and to offer certain capabilities. These are applied as appropriate: 'All of our schemes have a geometric basis whether it is the pinwheel arrangement of ... the courtyards in ... the tartan grid used at ... or the circle based geometry of ...' Studying the design work then reveals quite openly the precedents that have inspired these designs. Some are recent buildings, and some are historical buildings. Some may be from other objects such as the clinker built hulls of boats and so on. MacCormac explicitly refers to this process when on familiar typological territory as being based on the assembly of known 'tried and tested precedents'. In fact he goes so far as to use the word 'vernacular' when describing this process, and he clearly does not mean nor does he produce a vernacular style of architecture: 'Vernacular in the sense that each time you come to the problem you already have large elements of the solution. It's vernacular in the sense of process rather than product.'

It seems that the experienced designers share a certain kind of knowledge with which they structure their design process. This knowledge might be described as 'knowing what might work'. All have done the job many times and can thus think ahead. They foresee problems that they know are likely to be crucial or critical to solve for success. Far from expecting that they will simply be able to refine the design into detail later they anticipate the key issues and solve them first.

The 'situated' nature of design knowledge

Richard MacCormac's explicit statement that his practice adopts different design strategies for building typologies with which they are more familiar draws our attention to another important feature of design knowledge. In a brilliant critique of Artificial Intelligence Hubert Dreyfus (1992) relies upon a classification of intelligent activities into four categories or ascending complexity. The importance of this for us here is that Dreyfus goes on to argue that success in devising computer programs that perform tasks in one of the lower categories does not mean that automatically we shall be able to use the same techniques to simulate intelligence in a higher category. The reason for this will become more apparent as the argument unfolds but in principle Dreyfus argues that his four categories are not simply extensions of each other but are fundamentally different from each other in some important ways.

Dreyfus's first category is what he calls 'associationistic', and includes tasks such as solving a maze or word by word translation of language such as through a dictionary. We humans learn to solve such problems by trial and error and repetition. Computers can be made to solve them through decision tree techniques. The second category of intelligent activity Dreyfus calls 'simple-formal', and might include such simple games as noughts and crosses. Again we learn to play such games through experience and establishing rules which prove infallible. It is therefore possible to create algorithms around such rules to enable computers to play at least as well as humans. The third category of 'complex-formal' includes the more complex games such as chess. We have relied quite extensively in this book on research into chess playing since it approaches the complexity of designing and yet is amenable to more controlled study. We have seen that to learn to play chess requires more than the simple learning of the rules. It requires very significant amounts of practice, and that although some rules of thumb about how to play may be useful, they are not infallible as they are in noughts and crosses. We have also seen that expert players appear to work differently to novices principally by using pattern recognition techniques to replace otherwise extensive analysis. We have developed computer programs to play chess at least as well as grand masters now, but there is no evidence that they work in the same manner as human players. Computers of course can search vast databases so quickly that the need to replace search with recognition is less critical.

Finally then we come to Dreyfus's fourth category of intelligent activity which he calls 'non-formal'. This includes ill-defined games such as riddles, sensitively translating natural language and most importantly for us, design. Dreyfus argues that artificial intelligence techniques have not and will not lead to computers being able to work at this level of intelligence. One of the most important characteristics of the non-formal problem is its situatedness. This is a complex philosophical argument but essentially means that some essential knowledge needed to perform the task lies outside the problem itself but in knowledge of situations in which the problem may arise.

Riddles come into this category as quite specifically the rules by which they work are not laid down and the skill needed to solve them is a creative one of imagining the many unspecified situations in which the problem might occur and drawing solutions from them. The translation of natural language has turned out to be far more difficult a problem than was originally thought or might be suggested by the proliferation of computer word-check algorithms. It is relatively easy to get computers to do crude translation that will work adequately for the vast majority of situations but the ambiguity of natural languages is such that the remaining minority of situations remain totally intractable. Bar-Hillel (1964) has famously illustrated this by using the example of the word 'pen' which could in English refer either to a writing device or an enclosure such as might be used to keep small children safe while playing. Others have elaborated Bar-Hillel's example to produce even greater challenges but his initial example will suffice for our purposes here. If we see the sentence 'the pen was in the box' we automatically assume the reference is to a writing instrument. If, however, we see the sentence 'the box was in the pen' we assume the enclosure. The point here is that the information needed to make these two interpretations lies outside the actual sentence but in knowledge about pens, boxes, their relative sizes and situations in which they may coexist.

John Gero (1998) has pointed out that design knowledge is frequently similarly 'situated'. In fact of course design not only operates in the world but acts on that world in order to change it. Designers must be able to recognize and understand not just existing situations but ones that might exist if the design were to be constructed. In effect this means that a designer is potentially in some infinitely regressive world that shifts each time a change is made to the design. Thankfully most of the time things in practice are not really quite that bad or we could never reach a solution. However, design as an intelligent activity undoubtedly resides in this fourth of Dreyfus's categories in an undefined and shifting set of situations.

From this argument it may seem easier to see why design knowledge depends so heavily upon precedent or experience and upon an appreciation of the ways things could be, rather than upon rules or theories. Schön has argued that all design problems are unique. While this is theoretically true it is also misleading since most design problems have many features which they share in common with others. These features it seems we are more able to recognize through the possible similarity of potential solutions than through some abstract description of the problem. An ability to perform this recognition repeatedly in many situations and apparently without much effort then appears to be one of the chief distinguishing characteristics of truly expert designers.

The nature of design expertise

Taken together these five stages of cognitive development seem to account for the difference between novices and experts when it comes to designing. The stages logically appear in a sequence but each stage is probably not completed before the next stage begins. First, there must be the acquisition of the design domain schemata. Second, there is the development of a growing pool of precedent. Perhaps once these stages are fairly well developed we might think of a designer as being competent and professional rather than a novice or beginner. The next stage of design expertise is the identification of some guiding principles which develop over time and further structure and filter the continued acquisition of precedent. Once this has occurred a designer can become known for those ideas and may even be selected for jobs by clients because of the very presence of those ideas. It seems entirely appropriate therefore to use the term 'expert' for such designers. The next stage of developing the ability to recognize situations with little or no analysis and the final stage of building a 'repertoire of tricks' or design gambits which are integrated into the schemata used to recognize problem situations surely mark designers out as being 'masters'.

We have long used the word 'design' as both a noun to represent the end product and as a verb to represent the process. Only recently has the word 'designer' also become an adjective as in 'designer jeans'. The designers who can get work or sell objects simply because of their name are surely masters of their art or 'signature' designers. We may like their work or not, and this will always to some extent at least remain a matter of taste and values. It may also be that such famous name designers have been very opportunist or have creative and powerful marketing strategies and excellent connections. However, for them to remain for significant periods of time in such an illustrious position it seems likely that they have had to develop the levels of expertise we have identified and outlined here. Such expertise may not necessarily guarantee success then but it is probably a prerequisite in all but the most unusual or lucky cases.

It is interesting that the acquisition of experiential knowledge and the pool of precedent that we have seen here is a process that would be difficult to compress in time. Similarly the development of personal guiding principles is unlikely to be a rapid process. We have not attempted in this book to examine any personality correlates of expert designers although some studies of that kind were done some time ago (Mackinnon, 1962). There is thus no evidence here to say whether or not excellence in design can be the result of some inborn talent. Such a notion persists in many design schools and one frequently hears design tutors talking of 'talented students'. However, we have presented here evidence that firmly supports the idea that excellence is likely to be enhanced considerably through hard work and experience. Of course there must be some abilities that allow a designer to take advantage and make good use of all this experience. It remains the case that there are many design critics who must over a long career have gathered at least as much, if not more, experiential knowledge as practising designers, and yet are unable to achieve great things as designers themselves. It is also worth noting that designers seem generally to be fairly mature by the time they have acquired a significant reputation. Certainly if we compare designers with those excelling in sport, music or mathematics it is noticeable that the designers seem to take longer to become expert. It seems that in most cases Edison was right. Becoming an expert designer is probably more about perspiration than it is about inspiration, however glamorous and magical the latter might seem.

Bibliography

Adelson, B. (1981). 'Problem solving and the development of abstract categories in programming languages.' *Memory and Cognition* 9(4): 422–433.

Agabani, F. A. (1980). *Cognitive Aspects in Architectural Design Problem Solving*, University of Sheffield.

Aish, R. (1977). 'Prospects for design participation.' *Design Methods and Theories* 11(1).

Alexander, C. (1964). *Notes on the Synthesis of Form*. New York, McGraw Hill.

Alexander, C. (1966). 'A city is not a tree.' *Design* 206: 44–55.

Alexander, C. *et al.* (1977). *A Pattern Language*. New York, Oxford University Press.

Auger, B. (1972). *The Architect and the Computer*. London, Pall Mall.

Bar-Hillel, Y. (1964). *Language and Information*. Reading, MA, Addison Wesley.

Bartlett, F. C. (1932). *Remembering*. Cambridge, Cambridge University Press.

Benfield, E. (1940). *Purbeck Shop: A Stoneworker's Story of Stone*. Cambridge, Cambridge University Press.

Bilda, Z. and H. Demirkan (2002). 'An insight on designers' sketching activities in traditional versus digital media.' *Design Studies* 24: 27–50.

Bill, P., ed. (1990). *Building Towards 2001*. London, National Contractors Group.

Boden, M. (1990). *The Creative Mind: Myths and Mechanisms*. London, Weidenfeld and Nicolson.

Chermayeff, S. and C. Alexander (1963). *Community and Privacy*. Harmondsworth, Penguin.

Cerulli, C. *et al.* (2001). Capturing histories of design processes for collaborative building design development: field trial of the ADS prototype. In *Computer Aided Architectural Design Futures 2001*. B. de Vries, J. van Leeuwen and H. Achten. Dordrecht, Kluwer Academic Publishers: 427–438.

Chase, W. G. and H. A. Simon (1973). 'Perception in chess.' *Cognitive Psychology* 4: 55–81.

Chi, M. T. H. *et al.* (1981). 'Categorization and representation of physics problems by experts and novices.' *Cognitive Science* 5: 121–152.

Crawshaw, D. T. (1976). Co-ordinating working drawings, Building Research Establishment.

Cross, N. (1977). *The Automated Architect*, Pion.

Cross, N. (1982). 'Designerly ways of knowing.' *Design Studies* 3(4): 221–227.

Cross, N. *et al.*, eds. (1996). *Analysing Design Activity*. Chichester, Wiley.

Cross, N. (1996). Creativity in design: not leaping but bridging. In *Creativity and Cognition 1996: Proceedings of the Second International Symposium*. L. Candy and E. Edmonds. Loughborough, LUTCHI.

Cross, N. (2001). 'Can a machine design?' *MIT Design Issues* 17(4): 44–50.

Cross, N. (2003). The expertise of exceptional designers. In *Expertise in Design: Design Thinking Research Symposium 6*. N. Cross and E. Edmonds. Sydney, Creativity and Cognition Studios Press: 23–36.

Cruickshank, D. and P. Wyld (1975). *London: The Art of Georgian Building*. London, Architectural Press.

de Bono, E. (1970). *Lateral Thinking: A Textbook of Creativity*. London, Ward Lock Educational.

De Groot, A. D. (1965). *Thought and Choice in Chess*. The Hague, Mouton.

Dorst, K. (1997). *Describing Design: A Comparison of Paradigms*. Delft, Technical University of Delft.

Dorst, K. (2003). The problem of design problems. In *Expertise in Design*. N. Cross and E. Edmonds. Sydney, Creativity and Cognition Studios Press: 135–147.

Dreyfus, H. L. (1992). *What Computers Still Can't Do: A Critique of Artificial Reason*, Cambridge, Mass., MIT Press.

Eastman, C. M. (1970). On the analysis of the intuitive design process. In *Emerging Methods in Environmental Design and Planning*. G. T. Moore. Cambridge, Mass., MIT Press.

Eberhard, J. P. (1970). We ought to know the difference. In *Emerging Methods in Environmental Design and Planning*. G. T. Moore. Cambridge, Mass., MIT Press.

Fodor, J. A. (1975). *The Language of Thought*. Cambridge, Mass., Harvard University Press.

Fraser, I. and R. Henmi (1994). *Envisioning Architecture: An Analysis of Drawing*. New York, Van Nostrand Reinhold.

Frazer, J. (1995). *An Evolutionary Architecture*. London, The Architectural Association.

Gero, J. *et al.* (1998). 'An approach to the analysis of design protocols.' *Design Studies* 19: 21–61.

Gero, J. (1998). Conceptual designing as a sequence of situated acts. In *Artificial Intelligence in Structural Engineering*. I. Smith. Berlin, Springer-Verlag: 165–177.

Glymph, J. (2004). Panel elasticity modelling. Personal communication, B. Lawson. Langkawi, Malaysia.

Goel, V. (1995). *Sketches of Thought*. Cambridge, Mass., MIT Press.

Goel, V. and P. Pirolli (1992). 'The structure of design problem spaces.' *Cognitive Science* 16: 395–429.

Goldschmidt, G. (1998). 'Creative architectural design: reference versus precedence.' *Journal of Architectural and Planning Research* 15(3): 258–270.

Gordon, W. J. J. (1961). *Synectics: The Develpment of Creative Capacity*. New York, Harper and Row.

Groak, S. (1992). *The Idea of Building: Thought and Action in the Design and Production of Buildings*. London, E. & F.N. Spon.

Gross, M. (1994). *The Fat Pencil, the Cocktail Napkin, and the Slide Library*. Proceedings, Association for Computer Aided Design in Architecture, National Conference, St Louis.

Gross, M. (1996). 'The electronic cocktail napkin – a computational environment for working with design diagrams.' *Design Studies* 17(1): 53–69.

Hanson, K. (1969). Design from linked requirements in a housing problem. In *Design Methods in Architecture*. G. Broadbent and A. Ward. London, Lund Humphries.

Hertzberger, H. (1991). *Lessons for Students in Architecture*. Rotterdam, Uitgeverij 010.

Hodges, R. M. (1991). 'Opening the designers' spatial dictionary: the power of a professional vocabulary.' *The Journal of Architecture and Planning Research* 8(1): 39–47.

Jones, J. C. (1966). Design methods reviewed. In *The Design Method*. S. A. Gregory. London, Butterworth.

Jones, P. B. (1995). *Hans Scharoun*. London, Phaidon.

Lakoff, G. and M. Johnson (1980). *Metaphors We Live By*. Chicago, University of Chicago Press.

Lansdown, J. (1969). 'Computer-aided building design: the next steps.' *RIBA Journal* 76(4): 138–140.

Lasdun, D. (1965). 'An architect's approach to architecture.' *RIBA Journal* 72(4).

Lawson, B. R. (1975). 'Upside down and back to front: architects and the building laws.' *RIBA Journal* 82(4).

Lawson, B. R. (1978). The architect as a designer. In *The Study of Real Skills vol. 1: The Analysis of Practical Skills*. W. T. Singleton. Lancaster, MTP Press.

Lawson, B. R. (1979). 'Cognitive strategies in architectural design.' *Ergonomics* 22(1): 59–68.

Lawson, B. R. (1980). *How Designers Think*. London, Architectural Press.

Lawson, B. R. and J. P. Riley (1982). *ISAAC: A Technique for the Automatic Interpretation of Spaces from Drawn Floor Plans*. CAD82 Conference proceedings, Brighton, IPC Press.

Lawson, B. R. and S. Roberts (1991). 'Modes and features: the organization of data in CAD supporting the early phases of design.' *Design Studies* 12(2): 102–108.

Lawson, B. R. (1993). 'Parallel lines of thought.' *Languages of Design* 1(4): 357–366.

Lawson, B. R. (1994). *Design in Mind*. Oxford, Butterworth Architecture.

Lawson, B. R. and S. Pilling (1996). 'The cost and value of design.' *Architectural Research Quarterly* 4(1): 82–89.

Lawson, B. R. (1997). *How Designers Think*. (3rd Edition). Oxford, Architectural Press.

Lawson, B. and S. M. Loke (1997). 'Computers. words and pictures.' *Design Studies* 18(2): 171–184.

Lawson, B. R. (2001a). *The Language of Space*. Oxford, Architectural Press.

Lawson, B. R. (2001b). The context of mind. In *Designing in Context*. P. Lloyd and H. Christiaans. Delft, DUP Science: 133–148.

Lawson, B. R. (2002a). 'CAD and creativity: does the computer really help?' *Leonardo* 35(3): 327–331.

Lawson, B. R. (2002b). 'Design as research.' *Architectural Research Quarterly* 6(2): 109–114.

Lindsey, B. (2001). *Digital Gehry*. Basel, Birhhäuser.

Lloyd, P. *et al.* (1996). Can concurrent verbalisation reveal design cognition? In *Analysing Design Activity*. N. Cross, H. Christiaans and K. Dorst. Chichester, Wiley: 437–463.

Mackinnon, D. W. (1962). The nature and nurture of creative talent, Yale University.

Medway, P. and R. Andrews (1992). 'Building with words: discourse in an architects' office.' *Carleton Papers in Applied Language Studies* 9: 1–32.

Miller, G. A. (1956). 'The magic number seven plus or minus two.' *Psychological Review* 63.

Minsky, M. (1975). A framework for representing knowledge. *The Psychology of Computer Vision*. P. H. Winston. New York, McGraw Hill.

Mitchell, W. J. (1979). *Computer-aided Architectural Design*. New York, Van Nostrand Reinhold.

Mitchell, W. J. (1990). *The Logic of Architecture: Design, Computation, Cognition*. Cambridge, Mass., MIT Press.

Mitchell, W. J. (1995). *City of Bits*. Cambridge, Mass., MIT Press.

Mitchell, W. J. (1999). *E-topia*. Cambridge, Mass., MIT Press.

Mitchell, W. J. (2001). Roll over Euclid: How Frank Gehry designs and builds. *Frank Gehry, architect*. J. F. Ragheb.

Murphy, R. (1990). *Carlo Scarpa and the Castelvecchio*. Oxford, Butterworth Architecture.

Page, J. K. (1963). Review of the papers presented at the conference. *Conference on Design Methods*. J. C. Jones and D. Thornley. Oxford, Pergamon.

Peng, C. (1994). 'Exploring communication in collaborative design: co-operative architectural modelling.' *Design Studies* 15(1): 19–44.

Porter, T. and S. Goodman (1988). *Designer Primer for Architects, Graphic Designers and Artists*. London, Butterworth Architecture.

Rumelhart, D. E. and D. A. Norman (1983). Representation in memory. In *Handbook of Experimental Psychology*. R. C. Atkinson, R. J. Herrnstein, G. Lindzey and R. D. Luce. New York, Wiley.

Schank, R. C. (1982). *Dynamic Memory*. Cambridge, Cambridge University Press.

Schön, D. A. (1983). *The Reflective Practitioner: How Professionals Think in Action*. London, Temple Smith.

Schön, D. A. (1984). 'Problems, frames and perspectives on designing.' *Design Studies* 5(3): 132–136.

Schön, D. A. (1988). 'Designing: rules, types and worlds.' *Design Studies* 9(3): 181–190.

Schön, D. A. and G. Wiggins (1992). 'Kinds of seeing and their function in designing.' *Design Studies* 13(2): 135–156.

Simon, H. A. (1973). 'The structure of ill-formed problems.' *Artificial Intelligence* 4: 181–201.

Stokes, A. (1934). *The Stones of Rimini*. London, Faber and Faber.

Sturt, G. (1923). *The Wheelwright's Shop*. Cambridge, Cambridge University Press.

Suwa, M. and B. Tversky (1997). 'What do architects and students perceive in their design sketches? A protocol analysis.' *Design Studies* 18: 385–403.

Suwa, M. *et al.* (1998). 'Macroscopic analysis of design processes based on a scheme for coding designers' cognitive actions.' *Design Studies* 19: 455–483.

Tulving, E. (1983). *Elements of Episodic Memory*. Oxford, Clarendon Press.

Weston, R. (1990). 'Phased faculty.' *Architects' Journal* 191(5): 33–48.

Weston, R. (2002). *Utzon: Inspiration, Vision, Architecture*. Denmark, Edition Blondal.

Whitehead, B. and M. Z. Eldars (1964). 'An approach to the optimum layout of single storey buildings.' *The Architect's Journal* (17 June): 1373–1380.

Wilson, C. S. J. (1986). 'The play of use and use of play.' *Architectural Review* 180(1073): 15–18.

Zeara, A. (1995). 'Frank Gehry 1991–5, conversations with Frank O. Gehry.' *El Croquis* 74–5.

Zeisel, J. (1984). *Inquiry by Design*. Cambridge, Cambridge University Press.

Index

Page numbers for illustrations are shown in bold